ROSS HAMILTON

CYCLING IN
SURREY

21 HAND-PICKED RIDES

Bradt Guides Ltd, UK
Globe Pequot Press Inc, USA

AUTHOR

Having spent much of his life in the saddle, **Ross Hamilton** has numerous bikes cluttering up his garage. These include a 1980s Raleigh Pursuit which he used to ride to school – and which, decades later, he used to cycle from coast to coast, following the route of Hadrian's Wall. Ross has cycled all over southern England, from Kent to Cornwall. He completed RideLondon in four successive years to raise money for Guide Dogs and has also completed other famous rides such as the Nightrider (in London and Bristol) and the London to Brighton Cycle Ride. A former history teacher who has also worked in the heritage sector and run historical walking tours, Ross retains a particular fondness for his home county of Surrey, where he uses his local knowledge to devise unusual routes taking in cyclist-friendly cafés, sites of historical interest, nature reserves and picturesque views.

DEDICATION

To my wife, Sarah

FEEDBACK REQUEST

At Bradt Guides we're aware that guidebooks start to go out of date on the day they're published – and that you, our readers, are out there in the field doing research of your own. You'll find out before us when a fine new family-run hotel opens or a favourite restaurant changes hands and goes downhill. So why not tell us about your experiences? Contact us on ✆ 01753 893444 or **e** info@bradtguides. com. We will forward emails to the author who may post updates on the Bradt website at ⬦ bradtguides.com/updates. Alternatively, you can add a review of the book to Amazon, or share your adventures with us on Facebook, Twitter or Instagram (@BradtGuides).

FOREWORD

Rob Marshall, komoot

Surrey is a wonderful place for a relaxed bike ride, and this book shares some of the area's most beautiful routes, coupled with background features that fill you in on its history, culture and wildlife. Combine this with **komoot** – a convenient route-planning and navigation app that enables users to find, plan and share adventures based on riding type and ability. You can use the komoot smartphone app or ⊘ komoot.com, and it syncs with practically any GPS device and wearable.

By scanning the QR code that accompanies each route, you'll gain access to an interactive map and detailed route profile – an inch-by-inch breakdown of the surface type alongside an elevation profile, together with an estimate of how long the route will take you to complete, based on your fitness level. You can also save the route for offline use: komoot turns your smartphone into a navigation device, and when you hit 'start' on the ride the turn-by-turn voice navigation will keep you on track, meaning you can pedal in peace and soak up the views without stopping to check the map at every intersection.

Speaking of pedalling and enjoying the scenery, this Bradt guide gives you a wonderful overview of the places you're cycling through and recommendations for where to eat and sleep. Komoot's 'Highlights' (red dots on the komoot map) and 'Trail View' (green dots on the komoot map) can boost this intel with tips, insights and images from the community – recommendations for things that may not appear in the guidebook, like a hidden picnic spot or a section of road loved by local riders.

Ready to explore more with komoot and Bradt? Create your free account using the voucher code below.

DOWNLOAD A FREE MAPS BUNDLE TODAY

Download the Surrey and Sussex maps bundle for free at ⊘ komoot.com/g. Simply sign up for a komoot account and enter the voucher code **BRADTSS** *New users only. Offer valid until 31.12.2028*

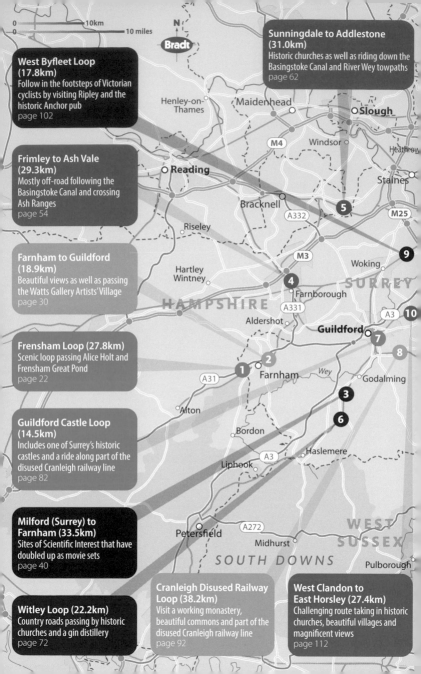

0 — 10km
0 — 10 miles

N

Bradt

Sunningdale to Addlestone (31.0km)
Historic churches as well as riding down the Basingstoke Canal and River Wey towpaths
page 62

West Byfleet Loop (17.8km)
Follow in the footsteps of Victorian cyclists by visiting Ripley and the historic Anchor pub
page 102

Henley-on-Thames

Maidenhead

○ Slough

M4

Windsor ○

Heathrow

Frimley to Ash Vale (29.3km)
Mostly off-road following the Basingstoke Canal and crossing Ash Ranges
page 54

○ Reading

Bracknell

A332

Staines

5

M25

Farnham to Guildford (18.9km)
Beautiful views as well as passing the Watts Gallery Artists' Village
page 30

Riseley

Hartley Wintney

M3

Woking ○

9

SURREY

HAMPSHIRE

4

Farnborough

A331

Aldershot ○

Guildford ○

7

A3

10

Frensham Loop (27.8km)
Scenic loop passing Alice Holt and Frensham Great Pond
page 22

2

1

A31

Farnham

Wey

8

Godalming ○

Guildford Castle Loop (14.5km)
Includes one of Surrey's historic castles and a ride along part of the disused Cranleigh railway line
page 82

○ Alton

Bordon

3

6

A3

Haslemere ○

Milford (Surrey) to Farnham (33.5km)
Sites of Scientific Interest that have doubled up as movie sets
page 40

Liphook ○

WEST

Witley Loop (22.2km)
Country roads passing by historic churches and a gin distillery
page 72

Petersfield ○

A272

Midhurst ○

SOUTH DOWNS

SUSSEX

Pulborough ○

Cranleigh Disused Railway Loop (38.2km)
Visit a working monastery, beautiful commons and part of the disused Cranleigh railway line
page 92

West Clandon to East Horsley (27.4km)
Challenging route taking in historic churches, beautiful villages and magnificent views
page 112

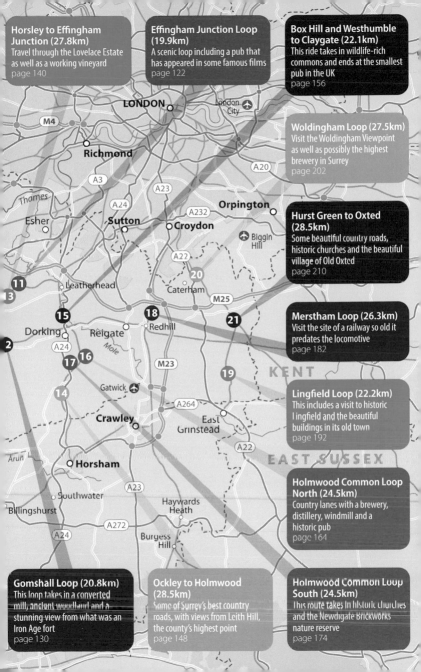

Horsley to Effingham Junction (27.8km)
Travel through the Lovelace Estate as well as a working vineyard
page 140

Effingham Junction Loop (19.9km)
A scenic loop including a pub that has appeared in some famous films
page 122

Box Hill and Westhumble to Claygate (22.1km)
This ride takes in wildlife-rich commons and ends at the smallest pub in the UK
page 156

Woldingham Loop (27.5km)
Visit the Woldingham Viewpoint as well as possibly the highest brewery in Surrey
page 202

Hurst Green to Oxted (28.5km)
Some beautiful country roads, historic churches and the beautiful village of Old Oxted
page 210

Merstham Loop (26.3km)
Visit the site of a railway so old it predates the locomotive
page 182

Lingfield Loop (22.2km)
This includes a visit to historic Lingfield and the beautiful buildings in its old town
page 192

Holmwood Common Loop North (24.5km)
Country lanes with a brewery, distillery, windmill and a historic pub
page 164

Holmwood Common Loop South (24.5km)
This route takes in historic churches and the Newdigate Brickworks nature reserve
page 174

Gomshall Loop (20.8km)
This loop takes in a converted mill, ancient woodland and a stunning view from what was an Iron Age fort
page 130

Ockley to Holmwood (28.5km)
Some of Surrey's best country roads, with views from Leith Hill, the county's highest point
page 148

CONTENTS

INTRODUCTION

Surrey is enclosed between Greater London and Berkshire in the north, Hampshire in the west, Kent in the east, as well as both the Sussexes to the south. It takes its name from the Saxon word *Suthrige*, meaning 'southern district', which dates from when it was part of the long-lost Kingdom of Essex; unlike some of its neighbours, it wasn't named after its inhabitants (eg: Middlesex – Middle Saxons; Sussex – South Saxons). Other times, it found itself part of the kingdoms of Mercia and Wessex before becoming the site (ie: Kingston upon Thames) where some of the earliest kings of a united England were crowned. During that period, the boundaries of the county stretched as far north as the southern banks of the River Thames – a clue to this is that Surrey Cricket Club play at The Oval in Kennington and the Surrey Quays at Rotherhithe, both now part of Greater London.

Surrey's borders started to diminish in the late 1880s with the establishment of the County of London, which took control of areas just south of the Thames, down to and including Wandsworth. The borders further eroded in 1965 with the establishment of Greater London.

The discovery of flint tools is evidence of human settlements in Surrey since the Palaeolithic period. The county has also been home to several major industries through the centuries, including pottery, glass-making, mining and wool. The latter was very important to medieval Surrey because much of the county's soil is more suited to grazing sheep than growing crops. During the Industrial Revolution, waterways and canals were built to help transport these goods up to the Thames for sale in London. With the Surrey countryside not having been converted to arable farming, the result is that there are large areas of common land to be explored, criss-crossed with a network of bridleways and footpaths. It can also boast of being the most wooded county in England: not for nothing is the county's symbol two interlocking oak leaves.

Surrey is a county of two halves. North of the M25 it is more built up, with many major roads, so there are not a lot of rides in that area. However, to the south we find the North Downs, the Greensand Ridge and the Surrey Hills. The Downs contain several habitats such as chalk grassland and heathland which support numerous rare species of flora and fauna, some of which you may encounter in this book. The Surrey Hills have been a designated Area of Outstanding Natural Beauty since 1958, and, thanks to the Green Belt, much of this part of the county has been protected from urban sprawl. There are plenty of challenging hills to ride up, but the rewards for doing so are well worth the effort. Not only are you treated with stunning views but you will be exploring peaceful country lanes with little traffic, picturesque villages, historic pubs and plenty of churches. You will also cross and ride alongside rivers and canals. The rivers you will encounter most often are the Mole and the Wey, the latter being the longest tributary of the Thames.

Surrey has a long history of cycling within its boundaries. To the fashionable cyclist of the late 1800s, the ride between Thames Ditton and Ripley was known as the 'Mecca for all good cyclists' (Ride 9, page 106). The Veteran-Cycle Club was founded in Ripley in 1955. In more modern times, the 2012 Olympic Road Race and the Prudential RideLondon have both passed through Surrey. Today, there are hundreds of kilometres of cycle routes throughout the county. Sustrans manages the National Cycle Network (NCN), and you will be following some of their signposted routes, namely NCN 21, 22, 221 and 224. You will also see signs for the 158km Surrey Cycleway, which was designed to take a circular tour of the county. There is also the 24km Yew Tree Way, which takes riders through areas not covered by the Surrey Cycleway, as well as the Planet network in and around Woking. You will follow some of the Saturn Trail, which shares a route with NCN 221, when you ride through Woking (Ride 5, page 62). Other routes which you may see signs for are Avenue Verte (a route between London and Paris), the Blackwater Valley Path (Frimley) and the Christmas Pie Trail. There are some off-road routes, too, including King Alfred's Way, a 350km round trip from Winchester which enters Surrey at Farnham and exits near Churt. To find out more about Surrey's cycle network, visit ⊘ surreycc.gov.uk and search for 'cycle network'.

The rides in this book take in much of the landscape that Surrey has to offer, so all you need to do now is to put on your helmet, choose a route and get on your bike. Happy trails!

CYCLING: THE ESSENTIALS

with Huw Hennessy

CHOOSING YOUR BIKE There's a wide and ever-increasing range of bicycles on the market today, including BMX, cyclocross, gravel bikes and fatbikes (great fun on sandy beaches). The routes in this book are suitable for the four most common and popular types (detailed here), and each chapter specifies which of these is the most suitable for that route.

Mountain bike (MTB) Strong frames, with suspension on the front and/or back wheels designed for absorbing the rough and tumble of MTB trails. Their chunky wheels and deeply treaded tyres give good grip on rough terrain off-road, but their weight and wide wheels make them less suitable for long-distance rides. I rode an MTB on those routes in the book that involve going off-road.

Gravel bike Essentially a cross between a road bike and a mountain bike, the increasingly popular gravel bikes are designed to go faster on all types of terrain. They are lighter and more aerodynamic than conventional mountain bikes, so are also good for longer rides. Most have drop handlebars, some with suspension, and a wide range of wheel widths and tyre treads are available, to suit your preferred ride. My regular companion rode a gravel bike on all the rides he joined me on.

Hybrid These have the speed of a road bike with the strength and gearing of a mountain bike. Hybrids are extremely popular, versatile, comfortable, sturdy and strong, with lighter frames and thinner wheels than most mountain bikes. They are better for long distances. I used one of these for most of the rides that didn't have off-road sections (as well as a couple that did).

Road bike Also known as a racing bike, usually with drop handlebars and made with lightweight material, such as aluminium or carbon fibre.

Ideal for speed and for longer distances on road, but with their narrow tyres and less robust frame than a mountain bike they're not so practical off-road on uneven surfaces. Touring bikes are sturdily built road bikes, with racks for carrying panniers. I rode one of these on some of the rides without off-road sections.

E-bike Electric bikes come in different shapes and styles, usually as hybrids but there are e-mountain bikes and even e-folding bikes too. They're great for getting up hills; most have an automatic power mode to give you an instant start or a manual override setting. You'll need to factor in the battery charging time for each ride. They're not cheap, but prices may come down as their popularity grows and, as the search continues for greener energy sources, will we all be riding solar-powered e-bikes sometime soon?

MAINTENANCE Keeping your bike in good working order is essential. Before every ride, take a few minutes to do the **M-Check**: a step-by-step assessment of the bike in the shape of the letter **M**. Start from the rear wheel up to the saddle, down to the pedals, up to the handlebars and back down to the front wheel:

1. Rear wheel: make sure it is firmly attached to the forks and turning freely. If using quick-release levers, check they are properly locked (facing backwards to avoid snagging on branches, etc). Run through the gears to make sure they're all working correctly.
2. Spokes: make sure they are all equally tight; pluck each one to check they sound about the same.
3. Tyres: check for possible splits, bulges and tears and remove any material stuck in the tread, which could cause a puncture. Ensure the tyres are inflated to the correct pressure (usually marked somewhere on the wall of the tyre).
4. Brakes: apply the rear and front brake in turn to make sure each grips the wheel firmly under forward pressure. Check there is nothing obstructing the brake pad and that it is not worn or loose.

5. Saddle: check that it is firm and that the seat post is not raised above the limit line. If needed, adjust the height and tighten the saddle with an Allen key or spanner. To measure your correct saddle height, you should be able to sit steadily on your bike, with the tips of your toes on the ground and your legs nearly straight.

6. Chain: keep it clean and oiled (though not too much oil as this can pick up dirt and debris, which can damage the chain set).

7. Pedals: spin them to make sure they rotate freely. Check that the cranks are firm and don't wobble or creak.

8. Front wheel stem: check that the handlebars and front wheel do not move independently from side to side. Do this by holding the front wheel between your knees and trying to twist the handlebars (not too hard or that will loosen them!). Tighten the stem bolt and handlebar clamp with an Allen key.

9. Headset: make sure it is correctly firm. Grip the head tube with one hand and squeeze the front brake with the other, and then try to shake the headset from side to side to make sure there is no loose movement or clicking sounds.

10. Frame: check for possible cracks or structural damage; this might occur at the joint between the head tube and the frame, and where the saddle post joins the frame.

11. Front wheel: apply the same tests as for the rear wheel.

EQUIPMENT AND ACCESSORIES For shorter rides, all you really need is a bicycle pump and a bell – and a lock if you think you might be stopping for a break along the way.

For longer distances, the following are also useful:

- puncture-repair kit
- inner tubes
- lights
- toolkit (multi-tool with built-in spanners and Allen keys saves space)
- tyre levers
- disposable gloves (to keep oil off your hands if the chain comes off, etc)
- fluorescent reflectors (ie: arm bands, spoke bars, ankle straps).

I had two punctures while researching this book and having these items in my kit bag meant it was not long before I could restart my ride. If you have any problems with your bike during a ride, there's a list of cycle-hire and repair shops on page 229.

WHAT TO WEAR As with the equipment, for short rides you don't need much; the only essential item, whether you're going off-road or not, is a **bike helmet**. In addition, for longer rides, the following are also useful:

- sturdy shoes
- loose-fitting clothing (including a lightweight kagoule even in summer, as the weather is unpredictable here, as it is anywhere in the UK; bright colours are good for visibility, but a word of warning: midges love them too!)
- gloves
- sunglasses or cycling goggles
- overshoes and gaiters (for muddy mountain biking and/or very wet weather)
- padded cycle shorts
- and, definitely last, stretched lycra tops and leggings (especially on colder days).

TAKING YOUR BIKE ON PUBLIC TRANSPORT There are two train operators covering Surrey, South Western Railway ($\mathcal{O}$ southwesternrailway. com) and Southern Railway ($\mathcal{O}$ southernrailway.com). Bikes can be taken on board but there is usually a limit of two non-folding bikes per four-carriage unit. Advance booking is not required but there are restrictions for non-folding bikes on trains arriving in London between 07.00 and 10.00, and those leaving London between 16.00 and 19.00. Both rail companies have a 'travelling with a bike' section on their website so check these before travelling. Unlike other areas of the country, you cannot take a non-folding bike on Surrey buses, and even for folding bikes it depends on how busy it is.

↑ Coffee stop at the Reading Room in Brockham (Amanda Thompson)

SAFETY Cycling is generally a safe and fun form of transport but is not without its risks and hazards. Following these guidelines, based on the Highway Code, will make your ride even safer for all:

- Be considerate to other users, taking extra care around those who may be short-sighted or blind, and people in wheelchairs or other mobility vehicles.
- Use your bell when necessary to signal to others you are approaching: don't startle people by shooting past on narrow paths without warning.
- Ride single file on narrow roads and paths.
- Give way to walkers, wheelchair users and horseriders, leaving plenty of room when passing each other in either direction. I have found talking to horseriders essential because some horses do not like bicycles at all and that could be danger to the rider as well as yourself.
- On shared paths and roads, show extra caution if cycling at high speed.
- Take extra care at junctions, bends and entrances, and signal when turning on to another road if other road users are nearby.
- Cyclists must follow the same traffic regulations as other users, including red lights, one-way roads and give-way lines.
- Narrow and high-banked country lanes muffle the sound of approaching vehicles, so always listen out carefully for traffic, especially on blind hills and corners.
- Be alert to parked cars on narrow roads in case doors open suddenly in front of you.

OFF-ROAD TRAILS There are ten rides in this book that use off-road trails: 1 (page 22), 2 (page 30), 3 (page 40), 4 (page 54), 5 (page 62), 8 (page 92), 9 (page 102), 10 (page 112), 11 (page 122) and 15 (page 156). If you'd like more information about the grading system used on off-road trails around the UK, see ⊘ forestryengland.uk/article/mountain -bike-trail-grades-and-safety.

HOW TO USE THIS BOOK

This book features 21 rides across Surrey, from Dockenfield in the west to Tatsfield in the east (with a couple starting in Hampshire and Berkshire). A pocket-sized guide cannot cover everything and I can't pretend to have included every route or place of interest to visit.

The routes range from 14.5km to 38.2km, and offer anything from a few hours' ride to a whole day out on your bike. They are aimed to appeal particularly to families and leisure cyclists who enjoy exploring not only the countryside but the history the county has to offer. We've also included rides over all sorts of terrain, with just under half including off-road sections. On these you might encounter mud, sandy soil or gnarly bumps to get you bouncing along.

Most of the start and end points are railway stations. Of the 21 routes, 12 are loops, which make travel arrangements easier. Of the other nine, six involve a direct train between the start and end stations. The other three involve at least one change (depending on the route you use to get back to your start point). Most of the routes are on well-established trails (such the NCN and the Surrey Cycleway), but with extensions and alternative routes to further explore Surrey and what it has to offer.

THE ROUTES For each ride, an **information panel** details the start and end point, distance in kilometres and approximate time to complete the route (depending on your fitness and number of stops along the way). Each has a **difficulty rating** (① easy or ② moderate) and a **scenic rating** (Ⓐ pleasant/interesting; Ⓑ great; Ⓒ superb), as well as an **overview of**

BEST FOR:

Families: 7, 9, 19
History and heritage: 3, 6, 7, 8, 12, 13, 14, 16, 17, 18, 19, 20, 21
Off-road adventure: 1, 2, 3, 4, 5, 6, 8, 9, 10, 11, 12, 15, 18, 20
Wildlife: 1, 2, 3, 4, 5, 6, 8, 9, 10, 11, 12, 15, 18, 20

terrain – whether the route is on- or off-road, if the path is surfaced, if any major hills are included, etc. I've listed which bikes are best suited to each ride. There is also a QR code and reference number to access a digital map on the navigation app komoot (see below).

At the end of each route chapter, you'll find information about getting to the start point, places to eat and public toilets. Unfortunately, there is a lack of local tourism centres in the county, the only walk-in one being in Guildford (see page 20).

MAPS Each chapter includes a map outlining the route and points of interest along the way. We have also teamed up with **komoot**, the route-planning and navigation app, to create a customised digital map for each route. These 'zoomable' maps also have detailed insights, including an elevation profile, way type and surface information, as well as photos of highlights and signage at key junctions. You can also use a smartphone to navigate each route, using the komoot app for iOS or Android. You may want to download the What3Words app, as there are specific points on some of the routes that can be found using this.

And, finally, for those of us who still like paper maps to see the wider picture, details of the relevant OS maps are given at the beginning of each chapter.

ACCOMMODATION See page 220 for a list of suggested hotels, B&Bs, hostels and campsites. Most of these are on or close to one or more cycle routes, and many have cycle-storage facilities. Some of the routes are away from towns and villages, but even the remotest corners often have nearby holiday cottages and cyclist-friendly campsites, with glamping pods, safari tents and shepherds' huts becoming an increasingly common feature of the countryside. Finally, **Visit Surrey** (visitsurrey.com) is the official tourism portal for the county, with comprehensive accommodation listings.

CYCLE-HIRE AND REPAIR SHOPS Considering Surrey has so many wonderful places to cycle to, there are very few places in the county where you can hire a bicycle. At the back of the book (page 229) is a list of

cycle-hire and bike-repair shops, with a number to indicate which routes they are closest to.

OPENING HOURS This book was researched and written in the winter to the summer of 2023. We have provided website pages so you can check when accommodation, pubs, cafés and other businesses will be open during your visit. All the establishments were open for business at the time of going to press.

FURTHER INFORMATION The only walk-in tourist centre in Surrey, **Guildford Tourist Information Centre** (155 High Street, Guildford, GU1 3AJ; ✆ 01483 444333; ✆ visitsurrey.com/Guildford) provides details about places to visit, tours and, most importantly of all, detailed local knowledge. The centre sits within Guildford House Gallery which has a dedicated exhibition space and a craft shop. Local museums are also a good source of information about their particular localities.

↑ Hankley Common (Sarah Hamilton)

1 FRENSHAM LOOP

START/FINISH	Bentley Railway Station
DISTANCE/TIME	27.8km/2½hrs
DIFFICULTY/TERRAIN	② Mostly flat; 40% of the route is off-road; some riding on sandy soil with some climbs; you will cross A-roads, and ride along B-roads and country lanes
SCENIC RATING	⑧ Woodland with off-road cycling on challenging rolling terrain of common and heathland
SUITABLE FOR	MTB, gravel or sturdy hybrid (with off-road tyres)
CYCLE ROUTE	King Alfred's Way, Shipwrights Way (NCN224), NCN22
MAPS	OS Landranger 186 (1:50 000)
KOMOOT REF	886103469

↑ Frensham Great Pond (Graham Prentice/S)

C rossing the Hampshire–Surrey border, you will be cycling on both on- and off-road routes which go through heathland including a Site of Special Scientific Interest (Frensham Common) as well as a forest where wood was once grown for warships. Some sections of this ride can be challenging, mostly because of the surface, which can be very sandy.

THE ROUTE

Although this route starts in Hampshire, I have included it here for three reasons: you will find that I like to start my rides at railway stations; it is not far from the Surrey border; and you will pass through some lovely countryside which you otherwise would not have seen.

Start this ride in ❶ **Bentley Station's car park**. To the left of the station building is a path over the railway lines. Cross over, making sure that no trains are coming, and turn left, passing through the white gate. You are now on the **Shipwrights Way** (NCN224). This 80km route links **Alice Holt Forest** to Portsmouth where wood was transported in the Tudor and Napoleonic eras to build warships. As the route slopes upwards, note on your right a carving of a butterfly. This is one of 20 on the Way in total, representing geographical, historical and natural features of the area, with three to see on this ride. This one is a silver-washed fritillary woodland butterfly, which makes its home in the conservation area that you can enter through the gate next to the carving. It is believed that part of the path we are taking is a section of a Roman road linking Silchester and London.

A kilometre from the station, you will cycle around a gate and on your left is the **Alice Holt Research Station** of Forest Research, the principal organisation for forestry and tree-related research in Great Britain. As the route bears to the left, turn right. After 500m, turn left, continuing to follow Shipwrights Way. You will soon come to the A325 which you need to cross. This is a busy road and I found it safer to walk across it. The route bears to the left but then quickly, at the trail post, turn right. After 700m, you will arrive at a gate. Pass by this and do not turn left into the car park but take the next left on to Hardings Road, ❷ **Alice Holt Forest Visitor Centre** will soon be on your right. Outside the entrance, you will see the second Shipwrights Way carving, this one of a chained tree. Trees were chained to determine the way they grew, moulding them into the shapes the wrights needed for specific parts of their wooden ships. It could take up to 50 years for a tree to mature into the correct shape.

Continue along Hardings Road until you reach the T-junction. Turn left and follow the trail for 1.5km. Pass the gate and you are on Church Lane. Look left and there is ❸ **St James's Church, Rowledge** which dates to 1870. The porch has three memorial panels in memory of those from the local area who served in and survived World War I. Look to the left of the porch to see a stone bench, ideal for a quick rest. At the end of Church Lane, you will see the **Rowledge war memorial**. Turn right on to School Road and then an immediate right on to Boundary Road, so named because it divides Hampshire and Surrey. The boundary is evident even without a sign because the road surface becomes noticeably worse in the area where the counties meet.

Follow Boundary Road for just over 2km until you come to a road sign for Batts Corner. You need to turn left just before the sign, and you soon come to **The Bluebell** pub (see below). A local told me that the small area of grassy land opposite the pub was where local criminals used to be hanged. Unfortunately, I have not been able to confirm if this is true or just a legend. This road finishes at a pair of gates but there is a trail to the right which you need to take. This trail takes you over **Bealeswood**

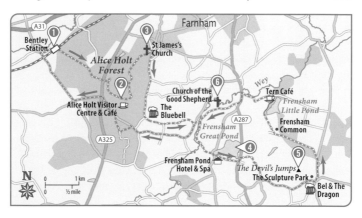

Common. A noticeboard, updated on a regular basis, details the flora (eg: common spotted orchid) and fauna (eg: sparrowhawk) that have been seen on the Common.

This route becomes Bealeswood Lane but do not follow this road as it bears right, but go straight ahead instead, following the trail which will come to a T-junction. Turn left on to Pitt Lane. Soon, you will need to turn right on to Mill Lane. You will pass over the **River Wey**, a tributary of the Thames. You will see a good deal of this river as you make your way through the book. Turn right through the gates and pass some buildings which used to be Fensham Mill. It might look as though you are going up a private driveway, but you can ride here. This becomes a narrow dirt track and follows the course of the Wey. When the trail starts to climb upwards, you need to be careful as this comes out on to a road. This is Bacon Lane and ahead of you is ❹ **Frensham Great Pond**.

Frensham Great Pond has its own beach which can be very popular during the summer, especially as you can go swimming (in designated areas only). Turn right on to Bacon Lane and then an immediate left on to Pond Lane, passing the **Frensham Pond Hotel & Spa** (see *Accommodation*, page 223). At the T-junction, turn left on to Farnham Road (A287) and then an immediate right, through the gate and along the trail. When a wooden fence appears in front of you, follow the trail as it bears left. The trail becomes a dirt track and ascends a short slope. There are some tree roots here which can make the ride a little bumpy. At the top, turn around and look behind you at the rather lovely view of the area you have just ridden through.

Descend. At some points, the trail becomes sandy. There will be a wooden fence on your right; when you reach the end of the fence, turn right. Continue along the bridleway and, after it bears around to the right, it will become a paved surface. This is Crosswater Lane. Follow this until you get to the junction, turning left on to Jumps Road. As you ride along this road, you will pass three small hills on your left. These are ❺ **The Devil's Jumps** (see box, page 27). At the end of the road is the **Bel & The Dragon** pub (see *Accommodation*, page 220) and opposite that is **The Sculpture Park** (✑ thesculpturepark.com) with its 650 sculptures and two miles of trails.

Turn left on to Tilford Road before turning left again at the red telephone box (which now houses a defibrillator) and on to Sandy Lane. After 1.3km, you will come to a ford. It does not look very deep, but I preferred to cycle on the footbridge. After 200m, you need to turn right on to **Frensham Common**.

Designated as a Site of Special Scientific Interest (SSSI), Frensham Common is home to all six species of British reptiles, which are: adder, grass snake, smooth snake, slow worm, common lizard and sand lizard. It is also home to birds such as the Dartford warbler and nightjar. I failed to spot any of these while I was making my way over the Common: in fact, I didn't have much success wildlife spotting on any of the rides while I was testing them for this book – hopefully, you will have more luck than me. The soil here in places is extremely sandy, making cycling difficult. However, these sections are few in number and do not last long, and the beauty of the Common makes up for it. As you bear to the right, you will see **Frensham Little Pond**. Follow the path, keeping the Pond on your right, and you will come to the **Tern Café** (see below), a welcome stop-off point with a great view over the Pond.

The trail bears to the left, and you then turn right through the car park where you will briefly join **King Alfred's Way**. Come out of the car park and turn left on to Priory Lane. Ride down this road for 1km and then turn left on to Farnham Road (A287). This is the busiest section of road on this ride, but you are not on it for long. Take the first right on to The Street; you are now entering the outskirts of **Frensham** village. The green is the home of the **Frensham war memorial** and of a red telephone box, which serves an interesting purpose: housing pieces of modern art.

Make your way through the village and on the right is the **Church of St Mary the Virgin**, dating to 1239, inside which a curious object is to be found. It is said to be a cauldron (or kettle) belonging to local witch Mother Ludlam (see box opposite, and Ride 2, page 37). The Street becomes Mill Lane, and you will be back at **Frensham Mill**. Follow the road to the right, crossing over the River Wey once more and turn left on to Pitt Lane which will become another road called The Street. There are

THE DEVIL'S JUMPS

The three hills that make up The Devil's Jumps stand out on the otherwise rather flat land around Frensham. The origin of the name has a couple of local legends attached to it. The first has it that the Devil was jumping between the hills which annoyed the god Thor. The Devil taunted Thor, causing the Norse god to throw a boulder in the Devil's direction. The boulder hit the Devil, causing him to fly away. The other is connected to Mother Ludlam's cauldron, which the Devil asked to borrow. Ludlam refused so the Devil stole it, making his escape by jumping across the common. Whenever his feet touched the ground, a hill sprang up. Ludlam gave chase and was able to retrieve her cauldron and placed it in Frensham Church for safekeeping (which is odd considering she was a witch).

↑ The Devil's Jumps (Gillian Pullinger/S)

a lot of roads called The Street in Surrey: why this is the case I have not been able to find out. You will be on this road for 1.4km.

You will pass through **Dockenfield** and see the ❻ **Church of the Good Shepherd** on your left. This church is quite modern compared to most in Surrey, having been built in 1910. It was designed by William Curtis Green, famous for designing buildings such 160 Piccadilly (London), once the showroom of Wolseley Motors and later a branch of Barclays Bank. At the junction, turn right and continue along Dockenfield Street. There is a path just beyond the first building you see on your left. Take this path (NCN22) and ride down it until you see the sculpture of a Roman pot on your right. Our third sculpture on the Shipwrights Way, this one commemorates the production of pots in this area during the Roman period: water, clay and wood for fuel were plentiful here.

Turn right after the sculpture and head up the trail until you reach Dockenfield Street again. Turn left. At the T-junction, you will need to cross the A325 once more. Take a left and then a sharp right on to Binsted Road – a fast downhill and a great place to freewheel. At the end of the

↑ Church of St Mary the Virgin in Frensham (Ross Hamilton)

road is **The Jolly Farmer** pub. Turn right at the junction and head along Blacknest Road. After 1.8km, there is a signpost for the station. Turn right on to Station Road and you will be back at Bentley Station and the end of the ride.

THE ESSENTIALS

GETTING THERE By train, Bentley Station is just over an hour from London Waterloo direct, or changing at Woking. Make sure you book tickets for Bentley in Hampshire and not the one in Yorkshire. By car, the station is 15km from Junction 5 of the M3 or just south of the A31 as it passes through Bentley.

FACILITIES Toilets are available at the Tern Café and the Alice Holt Visitor Centre.

WHERE TO EAT

Alice Holt Café, Bucks Horn Oak, Farnham, GU10 4LS; ✆ 01420 23540; ⌂ aliceholtcafe. co.uk. A mix of light bites and full meals, this has indoor and outdoor seating in a lovely country setting. Open seven days. £

The Bluebell, Batts Corner, Dockenfield, GU10 4EX; ✆ 01252 792801; ⌂ bluebell -dockenfield.com. Some light bites but mostly full meals, this lovely pub is best visited in the summer when you can sit and enjoy their rather lovely large garden. A good selection of beers as well. ££

Tern Café, Priory Lane, Frensham, GU10 3DW; ✆ 01428 681050; ⌂ nationaltrust.org.uk. Located next to a fishpond that once supplied the local bishop with his food, this café is welcome stop-off point halfway round the trail with a stunning view across the pond. It is open all year serving hot and cold light snacks, drinks and ice creams. Outdoor seating only. £

2 FARNHAM TO GUILDFORD

START	Farnham Railway Station
FINISH	Guildford Railway Station
DISTANCE/TIME	18.9km/1½hrs (two extensions; 1: 2.7km round trip, 45mins; 2: 7.9km round trip, 1hr)
DIFFICULTY/TERRAIN	② An undulating ride with a steep climb and uneven off-road sections; you will ride along some B-roads and country lanes
SCENIC RATING	© Picturesque villages with historic churches and other landmarks; beautiful vistas on The Mount
SUITABLE FOR	MTB, gravel bike or sturdy hybrid (with off-road tyres)
CYCLE ROUTE	Surrey Cycleway, NCN22, King Alfred's Way, Cycle Surrey Hills (Puttenham Loop)
MAPS	OS Explorer 145 (1:25 000)
KOMOOT REF	1019956484

This route follows the Surrey Cycleway and/or the NCN22, passing through some pretty villages. You will see several historic churches and one exceptional place of interest in particular (the Watts Cemetery Chapel). The views (especially from the top of The Mount just outside of Guildford) are quite stunning. Make sure you leave enough time to take them in.

THE ROUTE

Once you leave ❶ **Farnham Station**, head along Waverley Lane (B3001) and then turn left on to Broomleaf Road. This is part of NCN22, which you will be following, along with the Surrey Cycleway, for most of this ride. After 1km, turn left at the T-junction on to Lynch Road. As the road bears round to the right, you need to look out for a sign (on your left) for Surrey Cycleway and NCN22. Take the sharp left turn just after this sign on to Old Compton Way which soon changes its name to Moor Park Way. Follow this road, turning left when you see the sign for Moor Park Lane and the sign for NCN22/Surrey Cycleway. Continue straight along this road; when you come to the left turn, do not take it even though there is

← Waverley Abbey (SJMPhotos/S)

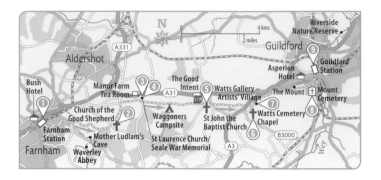

a sign for the NCN22. You need to go up the hill, along Compton Way, following the Surrey Cycleway for the next 4km. This is also part of King Alfred's Way.

Follow Compton Way until you reach the T-junction. Turn right on to Crooksbury Road and then a left on to Botany Hill (as an alternative, you can add Extension 1; see below). Follow this road as it climbs upwards, although you will soon be going downhill until you reach the crossroads. You are now in a village that goes by the name of **The Sands**.

Going straight across on to Binton Lane, you will come to ❷ **The Church of the Good Shepherd**. This beautiful little church was built, according to the sign above the door, in 1875. It is a shame that the extension that has been added to the back is not in keeping with the rest. You will see what I mean when you get there. Binton Lane takes a sharp left turn as you leave the village, and you need to be careful at this point: behind the hedgerow, on either side of the road, is Farnham Golf Club and the golfers cross at this point. 1.2km after this turn, you will reach a crossroads. Turn right on to Seale Lane. This is a busier road than the ones you have been travelling down previously. At the T-junction, turn right on to Elstead Road, following the sign to 'Elstead, Puttenham, Seale'. Behind this sign is a red telephone box which now houses a defibrillator. The road next to the telephone box is Wood Lane, which will take you to **Manor Farm Tea Room** (see below).

The route continues along Elstead Road, however, which then bears around to the right, and you'll see ❸ **St Laurence Church** on your left.

Like many other Surrey churches, this building was built in the Norman era, but restoration work was carried out in the Victorian period. You will come to notice the Victorians' enthusiasm for restoring old churches is a recurring theme throughout this book.

You can clearly see some of the Norman features, such as the pillars and the main door. Look out for the stained-glass window depicting Simeon and Anna (Luke 2:25–38); the information panel underneath tells you who the faces of those characters were based upon. Just past the church is the ❹ **Seale war memorial.** You can sit on the stone benches built into the surrounding wall, but you will have the first of many lovely views on this ride if you look in the direction of **Puttenham**, the next village along.

After the war memorial, the road bears to the left and becomes Puttenham Road, which you will stay on for 3.9km, although it changes

↑ View from the Seale war memorial (Ross Hamilton)

its name twice: to Seale Lane and The Street, respectively. As you make your way through Puttenham, you will see another red telephone box but this one has a display of photographs of the local area placed there by the Puttenham and Wanborough History Society. Just past the telephone box, the road bears to the left. This is the only place on this ride where I encountered parked cars in large numbers along the road, narrowing the available space for traffic. You will be joining the Cycle Surrey Hills (Puttenham Loop) at this point.

On your left is **The Good Intent** (see below), a pub with a depiction of Oliver Cromwell on it – something I have never seen elsewhere. Cromwell's government was infamous for banning all sorts of pleasurable activity during the brief time this country was a republic, but beer drinking was not one of them. As you continue along The Street, you will see ❺ **St John the Baptist Church** ahead of you. This Grade II-listed building, like St Laurence's in Seale, dates to the Norman period but went through some restoration work in the 1860s. Look out for an original lancet window in the southwest corner of the nave which the church believes dates to the 12th century. Outside, to the left of the entrance, is what was once the village well, although water has not been drawn from it since 1750.

Follow The Street until you reach the T-junction. Turn right on to Puttenham Heath Road (B3000) and then left at the signs for Puttenham Cricket Club and NCN22. The B3000 can be busy so take care when crossing it. You will be passing through Puttenham Golf Club on a track that has several pot-holes. After 1.2km, the track splits. Take the left-hand route, following the NCN22 sign (/// storeroom.civil.searcher). This track passes through some woodland and can be muddy but, when it becomes a paved road, turn right (/// lamenting.bonfire.dislikes). Follow this for 300m until you reach another T-junction.

Turn right on to Down Lane to visit the ❻ **Watts Cemetery Chapel**, which is on your left. This Grade I-listed building was designed by Mary Watts (see box opposite), with members of her pottery classes producing the terracotta decorations. Dating from the 1890s, the interior is covered in Mary Watts's artwork, the Tree of Life displayed on each wall, and is a

THE WATTS GALLERY – ARTISTS' VILLAGE

The Watts Gallery – Artists' Village was founded by George Frederic Watts and his wife Mary. George was an artist and sculptor, famous for his portraiture and allegorical paintings. In 1891 he and his wife had a house built, just outside of the village of Compton, which they called Limnerslease. There they created the Watts Gallery, which first opened in 1904. It was designed to showcase George's work but he died the same year it opened. Mary continued to live at the Grade II-listed house, the east wing of which is open to visitors. Mary created the stunning Watts Cemetery Chapel with the help of the local community, just down the road from the Gallery, where she painted a version of his famous 'The All-Pervading' artwork above the altar. The Watts Gallery – Artists' Village continues to support art through its community programme, and stages an annual exhibition by those who have taken part in the scheme. Booking in advance recommended for both the Gallery – Artists' Village and Limnerslease (⊘ wattsgallery.org.uk).

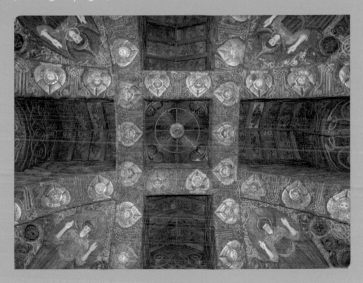

↑ The ceiling of the Watts Cemetery Chapel (AC Manley/S)

visual feast, not be missed. There are weekly tours (Friday, 11.00–noon); advance booking is recommended (🖰 wattsgallery.org.uk). The graveyard itself has a lovely cloister and, if you know where to look, you will find the gravestone of Aldous Huxley, author of the science fiction classic *Brave New World*. Look closely at the road signs in this area as some of them are on poles that resemble paint brushes.

Return to Down Lane, turning right and doubling back the way you came. Soon you will see a sign for ❼ **Watts Gallery – Artists' Village**, one of the few galleries in the UK dedicated to a single artist: that being the renowned Victorian Symbolist George Watts, husband of the aforementioned Mary (see box, page 35). Continue along Down Lane, which is a bit of a challenging climb. At the T-junction, turn right following the NCN22 sign and continue along Down Lane. At the next T-junction, turn right on to Farnham Road (A31), and immediately look right for a dirt track (/// tennis.melon.normal). There you will see a metal gate and a sign for NCN22. Turn right on to the track. As an alternative, instead of turning on to Farnham Road, you might want to dismount and walk along the pavement as the A31 can be very busy.

You are now on **The Mount** and you will be travelling along this track for 2.7km. After you pass around the metal gate, you will see a sign for **Henley Fort** on your left. Take the time to go through the treeline, left and/or right at any point for the next 300m, and you will see some stunning vistas. To the right is the south and the **Surrey Hills**. To your left and north you can see **Guildford** and **Woking** quite clearly. The large red building dominating the nearby skyline is **Guildford Cathedral**, which featured in the 1976 film *The Omen*. Be on the lookout for skylarks, which are said to be quite common here in the summer. Going through a gap in the trees at /// dining.legal.purely, you will see a small monument to the Cornish rebellion of 1497. The rebellion took place because King Henry VII was raising taxes for a war against Scotland, which the Cornish felt had nothing to do with them. With support of men from other counties, the Cornish marched on London. Before they arrived, they made camp in Guildford, where a skirmish was fought between the King's men and the Cornish. The rebellion was eventually crushed.

Continue along the track as it slopes downhill. Once you reach the paved road, look out on your right for ❽ **Mount Cemetery**. Not only does it have a lovely little chapel but you will also find the grave of Lewis Carroll. Helpfully, a sign will direct you to it, where he is buried under his real name of Charles Dodgson (see also Ride 7, page 88). After the cemetery, the hill descends rapidly, so reliable brakes are a must, especially as there will be a left turn before you get to the bottom. Turn on to Wodeland Avenue (as an alternative, you can add Extension 2; see below) and then right on to Wherwell Road. Cross over Farnham Road (A31) and on to Denzil Road. This has a gentle incline, and you will come down the other side of this by turning right on to Upperton Road. At the T-junction, turn left on to Guildford Park Road and, after 100m, you will arrive at ❾ **Guildford Station** and the end of the ride.

EXTENSION 1:
MOTHER LUDLAM'S CAVE AND WAVERLEY ABBEY

Instead of turning left on to Botany Hill, continue along Crooksbury Road, taking a right on to Camp Hill. After 600m (and near the base of the hill), there is a cottage on your right. Turn right on to the drive, which is also a public path. The owners of the cottage ask that you do not ride along their drive, so walk up to the gate and pass through. You do not need to walk far along the path until you reach **Mother Ludlam's Cave** (see also Ride 1, page 26). Ludlam is said to have lived here, but it was also a water source for **Waverley Abbey**. The cave today is home to three species of bats and entry is prohibited. Go back down the path, across the drive and turn right on to Camp Hill. At the junction, continue straight on Waverley Lane (B3001). As the road bears to the right, you will cross the **River Wey**, so watch out for swans who also like to cross here. You will see a brown sign for Waverley Abbey. Turn left into the car park, but do not continue along the road into Waverley Abbey House. This beautiful Georgian House is now home to a college and is not open to the public. From the car park, pass through the gate, making your way along the path before you pass through another gate. These gates are not designed for bikes and I had to lift mine over the second gate to get through. Ahead of you are the ruins of Waverley Abbey, which was founded in the 1130s. The ruins are now managed by the National Trust, and you can walk freely among them. Several films – eg: *28 Days Later* and *Hot Fuzz* – and TV programmes have used this as a location. To get back to the route, cycle back the way you came.

EXTENSION 2:
RIVERSIDE NATURE RESERVE (GUILDFORD)

Instead of turning left on to Wodeland Avenue, continue straight on to the bottom of The Mount. Avoid descending too quickly as you will come to a major road: Park Street. Cross over on to High Street and turn left into the car park. At the end of the car park is the entrance to a path following the River Wey, which you will be following for 3.5km. When you pass under the railway bridge, look left at the top of the entrance arch to the car park to see a train sculpture. You will need to cross over two bridges and major roads as the riverside path changes bank. You will reach a footbridge at **Stoke Lock**, which you may recognise from the front cover of the book. Stoke Lock itself dates to the 17th century when the Wey was opened to barge traffic, but what interests us here is what is on the other side of the footbridge. Through the metal gates is the **Riverside Nature Reserve (Guildford)**, an area of 30ha with four different habitats. There is a raised wooden path (which I advise you to walk along), allowing you to navigate the wetland area. There are plenty of flora (red campion and honeysuckle) and fauna (several species of butterflies and dragonflies) to be seen and, if you are lucky, you may even see some bats around sunset. Visitors are asked to stick to the designated paths. Finally, follow the trail back to Guildford and rejoin the main ride to finish at Guildford Station.

THE ESSENTIALS

GETTING THERE By train, Farnham is 55 minutes (with a change at Woking) from London Waterloo or 1 hour 2 minutes direct. There is a direct train from Guildford to Farnham which takes 23 minutes. By car, the A31 passes through Farnham. The nearest motorway junction is 4 on the M3.

FACILITIES There are toilets at both Farnham and Guildford stations. Public toilets are also found in Mount Cemetery, near to the chapel.

WHERE TO EAT

Manor Farm Tea Room, Manor Farm Craft Centre, Wood Lane, Seale, GU10 1HR; ✆ 01252 783661; ⌂ manorfarmtearoom.com. Housed in a converted farm building, this tearoom is open seven days a week, 10.00–16.00. A wide range of dishes is available including sandwiches and salads, as well as some main meals. Make sure you check out the craft shop next door. £–££

The Good Intent, 60–62 The Street, Puttenham, GU3 1AR; ✆ 01483 923434; ⌂ goodintentputtenham.co.uk. This old coaching inn has a lovely interior which includes a big log fire and a dedicated bike rail in the car park. Light bites are available at lunch only, but starters and bigger meals are available all day. £–££

The Tea Shop at the Watts Gallery, Down Lane, Compton, GU3 1DH; ✆ 01483 813590; ⌂ wattsgallery.org.uk. Open seven days, 10.00–17.00 (last orders 16.45), there is a good selection of sandwiches, cakes and scones. I particularly enjoyed the apple crumble cake. If you are really hungry, you can try one of their larger meals. £–££

3 MILFORD (SURREY) TO FARNHAM

START	Milford (Surrey) Railway Station
FINISH	Farnham Railway Station
DISTANCE/TIME	33.5km/3hrs (two extensions; 1: 1.4km; 2: 3.1km)
DIFFICULTY/TERRAIN	② Undulating or level; about 25% off-road on bridleways, some of which are sandy
SCENIC RATING	© Off-road trails, SSSIs and Nature Reserve with stunning views as well as historic structures
SUITABLE FOR	MTB and gravel bike (with off-road tyres)
CYCLE ROUTE	King Alfred's Way, Surrey Cycleway, Cycle Surrey Hills (Elstead Loop, Puttenham Loop, Devil's Punch Bowl Loop), Scholars Way (Extension 2 only)
MAPS	OS Explorer 145 and OL33 (1:25 000)
KOMOOT REF	1188849678

↑ Farnham Castle (Sterling Images/S)

O n this route, not only will you see some historic churches but you will also cross two medieval bridges. You will be traversing two Sites of Special Scientific Interest (SSSIs), one of which has appeared in several films. And you may also encounter some of Surrey's rarer wildlife.

THE ROUTE

Turn right out of ❶ **Milford Station** and ride down Station Lane. Turn right on to Church Road and then left at the roundabout on to Portsmouth Road (A3100). Turn right on to Chapel Lane and continue along here to the end of the road. Pass through the bollards and then turn right on to Eashing Lane. Once the treeline on your left has cleared, there is a brown sign for ❷ **Eashing Fields**. This site, created in 2020, is managed by the Surrey Wildlife Trust on behalf of The Land Trust. It is so new that visitors are asked to report any flora and fauna they see to help record the different

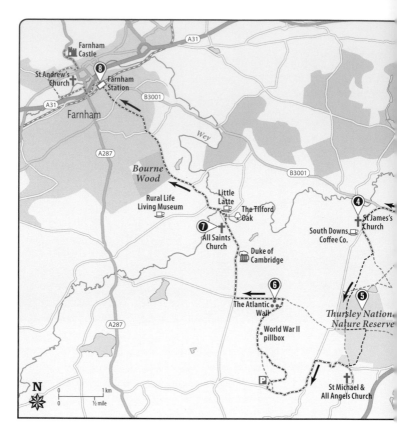

species that are making their home here. Turn left on to The Hollow. This road was once the eastern end of a Saxon defensive structure (or *burh*) built by Alfred the Great. It was located here to defend the Wey valley against the Vikings but the structure has been lost to history. As you come down The Hollow, you will go through the beautiful hamlet of **Lower Eashing**. Look out for **The Stag on the River** (see *Accommodation*, page 223) and what used to be mills next door. Mills have been on this site for centuries and at one time or another ground corn, or produced

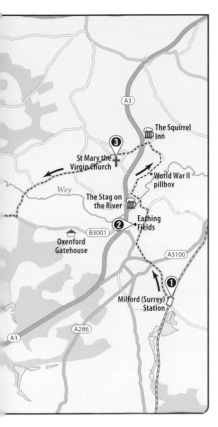

paper and then mattress stuffing. The current buildings date to the 1990s and house a business park.

Ahead of you is a medieval bridge, believed to have been constructed by the monks of Waverley Abbey (Ride 2, page 37), but there could have been an earlier structure here, considering the proximity of the *burh*. Cross the bridge over the River Wey and turn right down Greenway Studios. This is part of the Cycle Surrey Hills Puttenham Loop route. As you make your way along the track, look right and you'll see the remains of a **World War II pillbox**. These were built between 1940 and 1941 to defend against German advances in the event of an invasion; you will encounter a few of these on the rides listed in this book. Pass through the gate and the trail becomes a dirt track. The track is easy to follow but, at some points, the undergrowth has begun to encroach and you will need to be careful of stinging nettles and brambles. When you reach the track (which is known as Hurtmore Bottom), turn left. Continue along here and, when you pass through the tunnel, **The Squirrel Inn** will be ahead of you (see *Accommodation*, page 224). Turn left out of the pub and, at the T-junction, turn right on to Hurtmore Road. As you go under the A3, it becomes Elstead Road.

Further along the road is ❸ **St Mary the Virgin Church**, Shackleford, a Grade II-listed building. It was designed by Sir George Gilbert Scott, whose architectural works include the hotel at St Pancras Station and the Convocation Hall at the University of Mumbai. Constructed in the 1860s, this is rather a large church considering that the congregation is mostly drawn from local villages and hamlets. There is a challenge to be taken up if you like: visitors are encouraged to guess how many sheep are inside St Mary's. Here's a clue: look at the stained-glass windows.

Continue along Elstead Road for a further 2.8km. The road has a gradual downward slope, which does make this section quite an easy ride. The road will change its name to Shackleford Road just before you cross over the River Wey for a second time. Take a right at the junction, following the road sign for 'Elstead, Tilford, Farnham'. Turn right on to Milford Road (B3001) at the T-junction and make your way into the village of **Elstead**.

Take the left after The Woolpack pub, joining Thursley Road where you will soon see ❹ **St James's Church** on your right. Built under instruction from the monks of Waverley Abbey (Ride 2, page 37), who owned land here, the church has windows dating back to the 13th century. Currently, the bell-ringing team consists of one lady ringing all three bells at once, using one foot as well as her two arms. The route now becomes part of the Cycle Surrey Hills Elstead Loop. Continue along Thursley Road and you will pass **South Downs Coffee Co.** (see below). Just beyond this café, take the next left on to Red House Lane. Continue along here until you see a gate and then turn on to the track. You have now entered **Elstead Common** – a beautiful place to cycle but make sure you stay on the designated trails to avoid damaging the habitat and disturbing the wildlife. Most of the riding surfaces on the Common are made of sand, which can be difficult to ride on, but the following tips might help: (1) stick to the sides of the trails as the ground tends to be firmer here; (2) you should also see tyre tracks of cyclists who have preceded you and these tend to be (but are not always) on the most navigable sections.

You will be riding through trees at the start of this section but, when you emerge, the trail becomes quite narrow. This coincides with the necessity of passing over **Pot Common Brook**. Luckily, there is a small wooden crossing, but there are exposed tree roots on the trail descending towards it. I would recommend that more inexperienced riders walk this short

section. After the trail takes a left turn, follow it southwards. Along this section, there are signs for ❺ **Thursley National Nature Reserve**. Not only is this an SSSI, but it is also a Special Protection Area (for its breeding birds) and a Special Area of Conservation (for the habitats). Heathland was once common in Surrey but the conversion of land for human uses has rendered it quite rare. On the reserve you might see birds such as Dartford warblers and hobbies as well as insects such as black darter dragonflies.

Having crossed the brook, go another 1.8km and turn left (heading east) to join King Alfred's Way. In 465m, turn right (heading south), following the trail for another 1.3km when you will come out in the car

↑ Pudmore Pond in Thursley National Nature Reserve (Alex Manders/S)

park next to Thursley Cricket Club. Go through the car park and turn right on to Dyehouse Road – or left if you wish to visit Thursley Church (see Extension 1 below). Follow the road with its slightly uphill gradient until you reach the T-junction. Turn left here, going back on to Thursley Road and following the sign for Churt and Frensham. You will be following this road for 1.7km, which is where you need to turn right into Thursley

SURREY'S CASTLES

When William, Duke of Normandy, defeated Harold II of England at the Battle of Hastings, he may have won a kingdom but he did not win the peace. He had to deal with multiple uprisings against his rule, but he had only a limited number of troops, so to help secure his conquest he built a series of castles. The quickest building method was a wooden motte-and-bailey castle. The motte was a raised earthwork with a tower on top, the bailey contained the buildings used by the defenders, and the whole thing was surrounded by a wall and a moat. By the late 12th century, these wooden structures had either been converted to stone (eg: Windsor Castle) or abandoned, the only evidence remaining of their existence being the motte. There are ten sites in Surrey that could be designated as castles but, as you can see, three of these – Betchworth, Thunderfield and Walton-on-the-Hill – are open to debate.

1. **Abinger** One of Surrey's 'lost castles', of which just the motte remains (Ride 12, page 136).
2. **Betchworth** The crumbled ruins of a fortified 15th-century manor house (Ride 16, page 171).
3. **Bletchingley** Again, not a motte-and-bailey, but there is an incredible view from where the building once stood (Ride 18, page 190).
4. **Broomhall Copse** Another 'lost castle', and the most difficult to find (Ride 8, page 98).
5. **Farnham** Impressive and well preserved, visit both Castle Keep and Bishop's Palace and climb the Blind Bishop's Steps (see below).
6. **Guildford** A well-preserved 12th-century Norman keep (Ride 7, page 82).

Public Car Park. You are now entering **Hankley Common**, following the Devil's Punch Bowl Loop.

Hankley Common is another SSSI but it is owned by the Ministry of Defence, meaning that it might be in use for military training, which takes priority over public access. The Elstead Village website (⊘ elsteadvillage. co.uk) lists times of restricted access. I have seen the military on

7. **Reigate** The site of this castle is in the centre of the town and none of the rides go through there; the nearest are 17 and 18 (pages 174 and 182). None of the castle buildings remain today, as it was destroyed in 1648 during the Civil War. A mock medieval gateway was built in the 1700s and the grounds are now a public park (/// unless.drove.fired).

8. **Sterborough** Once owned by the de Cobham family (see Ride 19, page 192), this was originally a manor house on an artificial island, which became a castle after permission was granted by Edward III. The original castle was destroyed in 1648 during the Civil War. The island remains and a Gothic garden house was built there in 1754 using materials from the ruined castle. The site is now known as Starborough Castle and is privately owned. The nearest you can get is the grounds of Starborough Manor (/// ideas. older.guess).

9. **Thunderfield** It is debatable whether this is a castle at all. Looking at a map, you can see what looks like a moat filled with water. The ditches themselves predate the Victorian era which is when work was carried out to supply these ditches with water. It is on private land so cannot be accessed and was most probably a fortified manor house rather than a castle. The nearest ride to the site is 18 (page 182) (/// played.serve.herbs).

10. **Walton-on-the-Hill** Another doubtful candidate for the title of 'castle'. There is a mound here that could have been a motte, but the site has never been excavated. It may well have been just a meeting point for the freemen of the village. It is not accessible as it is on private land and the location is on none of the rides. Ride 15 (page 156) is the only one that goes close to this site, which is not far from the village of Headley (/// kick.rents.lovely).

manoeuvres when I have crossed the Common, so it is important to heed the 'no entry' signs, stick to the designated paths, and obey any instructions you are given by personnel in uniform. Access can also be restricted for location filming: the Common has been used for numerous movies such as *Skyfall* (where it doubled up as Scotland) and *1917* (France).

Go straight through the car park, past the gate and up the short climb until you clear the treeline. This dirt track bears to the right, then back to the left, and all the time you travel along it you will have some wonderful views across the Common. You will also witness the devastation caused by the wildfires that have plagued the Common over the years. Enjoy the sight of the gorse and heather, and keep your eyes peeled for fauna such as adders and nightjars. Also keep an eye out for examples of architecture from World War II. The first one you will come across is a **pillbox** (/// acted. movements.rust). The second is near your left turn at /// witless.tucked. mocked, which is also where the track turns to sand. (This can also be a bit challenging so stick to the sides and follow the tracks of other cyclists for the best route.) As you take the next left (/// awoke.putty.lurching), look to your left to see the ruins of a wall. These are the remains of a replica of ❻ **The Atlantic Wall**, the defences the Germans had placed on the French coast to defend against an allied invasion. Built in 1943 by Canadian troops, this was used by soldiers before D-Day to practise the storming of the Normandy beaches.

Follow the sandy track for a further 1km, passing the golf course to your left. At the crossroads, turn right on to Tilford Road; you will be on this road for 1.9km. Along the way is **The Duke of Cambridge** pub. On this site is Tilford Brewery, whose beers can be bought in the adjoining pub. Continue along the road and you will see on your left the Grade II-listed ❼ **All Saints Church**, built in 1867. Inside is a plaque dedicated to the memory of Diana Rowden, who died at the hands of the Gestapo after working undercover in occupied France during World War II.

Tilford Village Green is just past the church. On each of the green's three corners is an oak tree commemorating a British monarch, namely Victoria, Edward VII and George V. Follow the road as it bears right and, at the T-junction, turn left following the sign for the Rural Life Museum.

You are now on Tilford Street. On your right, you will pass The Barley Mow pub and, just beyond it, the **Tilford Oak**. Estimated to be 800 years old, the tree has had its trunk patched with iron sheets. At the next T-junction, turn right and continue to follow Tilford Street. You will soon see two bridges. Take the left one: not only is it a designated cycle route but it is one of two medieval bridges in the village. The road climbs gently upwards here and, when you reach the next T-junction, turn right on to Tilford Road.

You will be on this road for 4km. There are a couple of upward climbs but there is also a gentle downhill to compensate. You will also pass by **Bourne Wood**, which is managed by the Forestry Commission. The RSPB also work here and have had some success with the population of the Dartford warbler, a bird that almost died out in the UK in the 1960s. There are plenty of trails to follow through the woods, but not all of them are suitable for cycling. If you decide to do so, you might think you recognise some of the landscape, and that would be because numerous films have been shot here. These include a couple of Harry Potter films, Marvel productions such as *Thor: The Dark World* and, most famously, *Gladiator*. As you ride further along the road, the number of buildings starts to increase and that is because you are entering Farnham. Cross over at the traffic lights on the Great Austins–Merlin Way junction and, as the station comes into view, you will be briefly on NCN22. When you reach ❽ **Farnham Station**, you are at the conclusion of the ride.

EXTENSION 1: ST MICHAEL AND ALL ANGELS CHURCH, THURSLEY

As you leave Elstead Common through the car park, turn left on to Dyehouse Road and you will be passing through **Thursley** village. It is believed that its name comes from 'Thor's lee'. Thor is the Norse God of many things including lightning and storms, as well as trees; 'lee' comes from the Old English word *leah*, which means wood or clearing. It is believed that Thor was worshipped here, and in fact there is a representation of the god on the village sign. Noted architect Edwin Lutyens lived in Thursley during his childhood and he designed buildings all over the UK, including several in Surrey such as Goddards (Abinger;

see Ride 12, page 135), Munstead Wood (Busbridge), Orchards (Bramley) and Tigbourne Court (Wormley). Unfortunately, most of these buildings are in private hands and cannot be visited (and he didn't design any of Thursley's buildings). Once described as 'the greatest British architect of the twentieth (or of any other) century', he also completed several other works in the UK and around the world including Baroda House in New Delhi and the Villers-Bretonneux Australian National Memorial in France.

Turn right on to The Street and you will see the aforementioned village sign. Follow the road until it bears around to the right, becoming Highfield Lane. On your right is **St Michael and All Angels Church**. There is so much to see in this Grade I-listed building that it could have had a chapter all to itself, but here are some things to look out for. Two of its windows are believed to date back to Anglo-Saxon times. Look up at the spire and you can see a sundial; its Latin inscription 'Hora Pars Vitae' means 'every hour is a part of life'. You will also notice that the vestry has a glass screen across it: a beautiful piece of work, full of symbolism. The tree in the image is a

↑ Church of St Michael and All Angels, Thursley (Peter S/WC)

birch, which are to be seen in abundance on nearby Thursley Common. The flames at bottom left allude to the massive fire which badly afflicted the Common in 2006. The signs of life at the top of the tree represent the Common's all-important regeneration.

As well as the obligatory yew trees (one of which is nicknamed 'Bart Simpson' due to its resemblance to that character's hairstyle), the churchyard contains a wooden building which was once the village school. Walking around, look out for the graves of Natalie Wick, a survivor of the *Titanic*, and the Unknown Sailor. The latter was an unfortunate member of the Navy, returning to Portsmouth from London in 1786. Thursley was one of his stops and here he was befriended by three other sailors at the Red Lion inn. This friendship was short-lived: the Unknown Sailor clearly had plenty of money and his new companions wanted it for themselves. The quartet left together; when they thought they were unseen, the three men murdered the poor sailor, robbing him of his clothes and money before dumping his body. However, witnesses did come forward and the men were soon arrested. Found guilty of murder, the three were hanged at a site near the scene of the crime. His gravestone – paid for by public subscription as, even to this day, no-one knows his name or where he was from – depicts the act of murder. Look also for a 'leaping board', a bed-head-shaped grave marker used instead of a stone – a rare feature in churches because they were made of wood and tend to rot away. Near it is a bench, which is a great spot to relax and enjoy the view. Follow the route back to rejoin the ride.

EXTENSION 2: FARNHAM AND ITS CASTLE

Farnham is a beautiful town, and here is also an opportunity to visit one of Surrey's ten castles. When you reach Farnham Station, take an immediate left on to Approach Road. Follow this for 460m and, at the T-junction, turn right on to Firgrove Hill (A287). Take the second left on to Red Lion Lane which becomes Weydon Mill Lane. At the end of the lane, take a right and follow the footpath over the bridge. This crosses the River Wey and into **Bishops Meadow**. Follow the footpath across the park and on to Whitlet Close. Instead of bearing right as it becomes Crosby Way, follow the Mead Lane path. At the T-junction, turn right on to West Street (A325) and then left on to Potters Gate which is part of Scholars Way. The first part of this road is cobbled so I hope you are wearing padded cycle shorts! At the end of the road, turn right on to Falkner Road and, at the next junction, bear left on to Long Garden Way. Follow the road until you reach The Hop Blossom pub, when this becomes a footpath called Long Garden Walk. At the end of the path, turn left on to Castle Street. Follow this as it goes uphill, and the castle is on your right.

Farnham Castle was built in the 1100s and was home to the Bishop of Winchester for over 800 years. The **Castle Keep** is open every day (except when there is a private function) and the **Bishop's Palace** is open Wednesday afternoons (14.00–16.00). You may also wish to climb the **Blind Bishop's Steps**. These were built for Richard Fox so he could walk from the town up to the castle after his eyesight began to fail. The bishop needed to count his steps as he walked, so there are seven steps, followed by a level which can be covered in seven strides; and this arrangement is itself repeated seven times.

Farnham town is also worth a visit, including the **Museum of Farnham** at 38 West Street located in an 18th-century town house. You should also pay a visit to **St Andrew's Church** on Lower Church Lane, which is one of the bigger churches I have visited in Surrey. There was a church here in the Anglo-Saxon period but the oldest existing parts date to the 12th century. The glass in the east window was designed by Augustus Pugin, one of the architects responsible for the current Palace of Westminster. There are numerous pubs, including one named after William Cobbett. Born in Farnham, Cobbett's legacy is as a radical politician, political journalist and author of the book *Rural Rides* (nothing to do with bicycles, unfortunately; Cobbett's mode of transport was a horse). You will find his grave at St Andrew's.

THE ESSENTIALS

GETTING THERE By train, Milford (Surrey) is a 53-minute journey from London Waterloo. By car, exit the A3 at the Milford Junction turning. To return to Milford, catch a train from Farnham via Guildford.

FACILITIES Toilets are on Milford and Farnham stations (but only when the ticket office is open), and in The Hart, a road off West Street in Farnham.

WHERE TO EAT

South Downs Coffee Co., 172 Thursley Rd, Elstead, GU8 6DH; ☎ 01252 702323; 🖥 172elstead.southdownscoffee.co.uk. This café has the cyclist in mind, with a pump, dedicated water station and protein powder available. Breakfast and lunch menus offering a selection of light bites, cakes and hot and cold drinks (I really enjoyed the vanilla-caramel smoothie) are also available. A selection of local produce such as honey can also be purchased to take away (Tue–Fri 08.00–16.00; Sun–Mon 09.00–15.00). **£**

Little Latte Tilford, Tilford St, Tilford, GU10 2BU; ☎ 01252 854052; 🖥 littlelatte.co.uk. Located next to The Barley Mow pub, it serves a selection of light bites (eg: panini and baps)

along with various drinks and homemade cakes (Wed–Sun 08.00–16.30; closed Mon & Tues). **£**

The Market Garden Café, Rural Life Living Museum, Reeds Rd, Tilford, GU10 2DL; ☎ 01252 795571; 🖥 rural-life.org.uk. Located on the site of the Rural Life Living Museum, the café can be visited without a museum ticket. Offers b/fast and lunch options as well as light bites such as panini and jacket potatoes. There is a selection of hot and cold drinks as well as homemade cakes. Closed Tue & Wed but open seven days during Surrey school holidays. Look out for the bike-shaped cycle racks and you might also see one of the museum's narrow-gauge steam trains on your visit. **£–££**

4 FRIMLEY TO ASH VALE

START	Frimley Railway Station
FINISH	Ash Vale Railway Station
DISTANCE/TIME	29.3km/3hrs (extension: 2.9km round trip, 15mins)
DIFFICULTY/TERRAIN	② Paved roads, plus several off-road trails with some steep climbs on sandy soil
SCENIC RATING	⑧ Nature reserve on Ash Ranges, Basingstoke Canal towpath, and farmland
SUITABLE FOR	MTB, gravel bike or sturdy hybrid (with off-road tyres)
CYCLE ROUTE	Basingstoke Canal towpath, Blackwater Valley Path South, Blackwater Valley Red Route, Christmas Pie Trail
MAPS	OS Explorer 145 (1:25 000)
KOMOOT REF	1026770781

↑ Anglers' Flash on the Basingstoke Canal at Ash Vale (BabelStone/WC)

A scenic ride, but one for the more experienced rider as it is a 50/50 split of on- and off-road sections. The latter include Ash Ranges Nature Reserve, the Basingstoke Canal and the Blackwater Valley paths. You will need to ensure that Ash Ranges is open before attempting this ride as it is owned by the Ministry of Defence and not accessible to the public at certain times. These tend to be weekday daytimes but can include weekends as well. If you arrive at the gates to the Ranges to find them locked with a red flag on one of the flagpoles, you will not be able to enter. To find out if Ash Ranges is open on a particular day, go to ⊘ gov.uk/government/publications/south-east -training-estate-firing-times or ✆ 01420 483405.

THE ROUTE

To exit ❶ **Frimley Railway Station**, follow the road (Station Approach) and then turn left on to Frimley High Street. Go over the bridge and at the top you will see a sign for a cycle lane and Blackwater Valley Path South. Join the cycle lane and pass through the gate. You will see the **Blackwater River** on your right and several small lakes on your left. This area teems with wildlife: birds such as coots are attracted to the dragonflies, damselflies and other invertebrates. After 1.3km, pass through another gate and turn left on to The Hatches. After 450m, you will reach an unmanned railway crossing so please ensure no trains are coming before walking across this.

Continue along The Hatches until it becomes The Green. Turn left on to Sturt Road (B3411) and then turn right at the roundabout on to Guildford Road (B3012). These B-roads can be busy, but you will not be on them for long. Pass over the railway bridge and on your left is The King's Head (Harvester). Do not go over the next bridge but head down the path on your right. This will take you to the **Basingstoke Canal**. Turn right and follow the towpath for 3km.

The canal was opened in 1794 and, like most canals in this country, it has a towpath alongside it. Canals were built before the advent of the motor engine so the most efficient way of transporting goods on the canal boats was for them to be towed by a horse. Over the years, this canal fell into disrepair and by 1932 it was closed. Only after many years of restoration work by a dedicated army of volunteers did the canal reopen. It is now

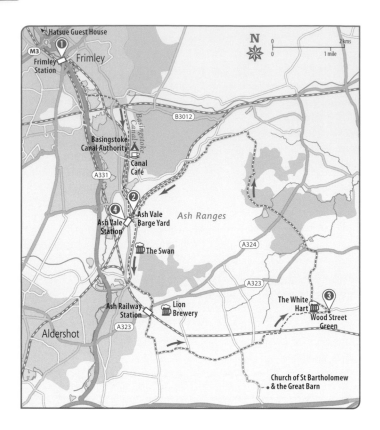

owned by Surrey and Hampshire councils, who formed a canal authority to manage the waterway. Some sections (including Woking on Ride 5, page 62) are now Sites of Special Scientific Interest. There are 24 different species of dragonflies along this canal, including the chaser dragonfly.

Having passed under the third bridge, you will glimpse a corrugated-iron building. This used to be ❷ **Ash Vale Barge Yard**, a workshop that built and repaired canal boats. Turn right before the building, turning right again to cross the bridge. Follow the trail as it bears to the left. As the gradient increases, you will pass a **World War II pillbox**. Pass through the gate and on to **Ash Ranges**. Remember: if you cannot open the gate, do not enter the grounds.

Although Ash Ranges is owned by the Ministry of Defence, it is managed by the Surrey Wildlife Trust. This is because the heathland is home to many rare species of invertebrates (green tiger beetle), reptiles (sand lizard) and plants (the carnivorous *Drosera*, more commonly known as a sundew). Follow the route for 4km as it climbs up some challenging sandy slopes. My advice is to ride along the sides where the ground can be firmer. The route takes a right turn after a red-brick building; after 1.4km, go through the gate to leave Ash Ranges and turn right. After 1km, you reach another gate. Don't go through here but take a left and follow this trail, which can be very muddy after heavy rainfall. At the end of the trail is a wooden fence. When you see it, turn right and then left on to Henley Gate. Cross over Aldershot Road (A324) and on to Cobbett Hill Road. At the end of this road, turn left on to a different Aldershot Road (A323) and, shortly afterwards, turn right into Frog Grove Lane, which is bordered by signs welcoming you to **Wood Street Village**.

↑ World War II pillbox near Ash Ranges (Ross Hamilton)

THE PILGRIM'S WAY

The Pilgrim's Way is said to be a series of ancient walkways used in the Middle Ages by pilgrims going between Winchester and Canterbury. Winchester had been an important city since Anglo-Saxon times, and a cathedral was built there by the Normans. Canterbury had its own cathedral which housed the shrine of Thomas Becket, making it an important destination for pilgrims prior to the dissolution of the monasteries in Henry VIII's reign. But with the shift from Catholicism to Protestantism, the practice of venerating saints came to an end and the Pilgrim's Way was forgotten. With the growth of leisure time during the Victorian era, and an increased interest in history, walking routes once trodden by pilgrims became fashionable – but by this time some of those routes had become major highways. The North Downs Way was created to offer modern walkers (and indeed cyclists) a similar experience to those who once followed the Pilgrim's Way.

↑ Riding the North Downs Way on Reigate Hill (SJ Images/A)

You will continue on this road for 1.8km, when ❸ **Wood Street Green** will be ahead of you: turn right on to the road of the same name. Look left over the green and you will see the last remaining **maypole** in Surrey. It was erected to celebrate the Coronation of Elizabeth II in 1953 and the green hosts fairs in the spring and summer.

Turn right on to White Hart Lane, passing **The White Hart** pub. Continue along the track and, after passing Wood Street Village Cricket Club, you will join the Christmas Pie Trail, distinguishable by the Christmas pudding illustrations along the trail. 1.1km after the Cricket Club, you will pass under a railway arch. Take a sharp right and you will soon come to Flexford Road. The road bears to the right and you will come to a junction. Head straight on, following the sign for the Christmas Pie Trail and continuing down Flexford Road. This is the hamlet of **Christmas Pie** which gets its name from a family that lived in the area (and who still own a bakery in nearby Worplesdon with another branch along this route in Ash Vale; see below). The 'pie' comes from an Anglo-Saxon word, *pightle*, which translates as 'small piece of arable land'. Turn left here for the extension (see below).

At the crossroads, go straight over Westwood Lane and on to Green Lane East. Continue for 1.7km (as it becomes Green Lane West) and then take the first left turning you come to. You will know you are on the right path because you will see a pond with a duck house on your left. You are now on Ash Green Lane East. You will soon see some buildings on your left and the road is paved. At the crossroads, turn right on to White Lane. You will shortly cross a bridge and, if you look down, you will catch sight of what used to be a railway line that passed through here. This was part of the **Tongham line** but it closed to passengers in 1937 and to goods in 1960. The building on your right is the former **Ash Green Halt Station** which is now a private residence.

The road bears round to the left and becomes Foreman Road. Follow this for 800m until you reach the T-junction. Ahead of you is **Ash Railway Station**. Turn right on to Guildford Road (A323). At the first roundabout, take the first exit on to Ash Hill Road (B3411). At the next roundabout, take the second exit on to Vale Road. Once you pass over the bridge, turn right, and rejoin the Basingstoke Canal towpath. Follow this for 2km until you come to the Ash Vale Barge Yard you passed earlier. Turn left here, riding along Station Approach; the entrance to ❹ **Ash Vale Railway Station** is on your right. If you still have the energy and would like to ride a further 6km, you can retrace your steps back to Frimley Station.

EXTENSION: THE GREAT BARN AND CHURCH OF ST BARTHOLOMEW, WANBOROUGH

The hamlet of **Wanborough** is home to the oldest wooden building in Surrey: the **Great Barn**. Built in 1388 by local monks, the barn is open to the public but only on certain days (check ⌀ wanboroughgreatbarn. co.uk for availability). You can also visit the **Church of St Bartholomew**. There is evidence that there has been a church on this site since the days of Edward the Confessor (ruled 1042–66). The land around the church was used for sheep farming and the Great Barn was constructed to store the wool, a major source of income in England in the Middle Ages. The church was a stopping point on the **Pilgrim's Way** (see box, page 58).

↑ The Great Barn at Wanborough (John Armagh/WC)

To get there, turn left at the end of Flexford Road and on to Westwood Lane. Cycle for 1.5km and then take another left at the wooden sign for Wanborough. To get back to the ride route, just come back the way you came.

THE ESSENTIALS

GETTING THERE By train, Frimley Station is just over an hour from London Waterloo, changing at Ash Vale. By car, the station is 1.3km from Junction 4 of the M3, along the A331, A325 and then Frimley High Street.

FACILITIES There are public toilets at the Basingstoke Canal Authority and next to the Rose and Thistle pub, Sturt Road, Frimley Green. There are also toilets on Ash Vale Station.

WHERE TO EAT

Canal Café, off Mytchett Heath, Mytchett GU16 6DE; ✆ 01252 521800. A lovely stop-off next to the Basingstoke Canal. Salads, burgers, b/fasts and light bites are available, along with hot and cold drinks. **£**

The Swan, 2 Hutton Rd, Ash Vale, GU12 5HA; ✆ 01252 325212; ⌖ chefandbrewer.com. A wide range of meals as well as a selection of lighter bites. As it is not far from Ash Vale, you can walk your bike to the station if you fancy something more substantial after the ride. **££**

Christmas Bakery, 9a Wharf Rd, Ash Vale, GU12 5AZ; ✆ 01252 316552; ⌖ christmas -bakery.co.uk. A family-run business since 1860, the bakery offers a substantial range of products to take away. This includes pasties, sausage rolls, baguettes and sandwiches. Hot and cold drinks are also available **£**

5 SUNNINGDALE TO ADDLESTONE

START	Sunningdale Railway Station
FINISH	Addlestone Railway Station
DISTANCE/TIME	31km/2½hrs
DIFFICULTY/TERRAIN	② Flat for most of the ride following B-roads, with 60% on towpaths or off-road tracks
SCENIC RATING	⑧ Country roads, canal and river towpaths, World War II pillbox, woodland and a common
SUITABLE FOR	MTB, gravel or sturdy hybrid (with off-road tyres)
CYCLE ROUTE	Basingstoke Canal Towpath, Saturn Trail (NCN221)
MAPS	OS Explorer 160 and 145 (1:25 000)
KOMOOT REF	889266827

S tarting off just over the border in Berkshire, your journey takes you through Chobham Common, a Site of Special Scientific Interest, and the historic village of Chobham. As well as seeing some interesting old churches, you will be riding along the Basingstoke Canal and River Wey towpaths.

THE ROUTE

Although this route starts in the village of Sunningdale (Berkshire), I have included it here because it is just over the county border and the station is the nearest one to the northernmost section of Chobham Common.

Once you leave ❶ **Sunningdale Station**, you will be on London Road (A30). Turn left and, not long afterwards, turn right on to Chobham Road (B383). The A30 can be busy so please be careful. After passing through **Sunningdale** village, you will soon be cycling over a railway bridge. As you come down the other side of the bridge, you will also notice that the train line disappears behind a line of trees and, for the next 4.5km, you will be cycling through **Chobham Common**. You also pass a sign welcoming you to Surrey.

Chobham Common is managed by the Surrey Wildlife Trust, who recommend visiting it in the summer months when the vegetation is at is most spectacular and you will see the greatest variety of animals.

← Coxes Lock in Addlestone (Ross Hamilton)

A visit to their website (surreywildlifetrust.org) will give you an idea of the variety of flora (bell heather/round-leaved sundew) and fauna (slow worm/yellowhammer) to be seen. There are plenty of trails through the Common: if you decide to ride them, I recommend a sturdy bike with plenty of grip on the tyres. Some of the trails are very narrow, so please stick to the larger main paths to avoid disturbing sensitive wildlife. You will find these trails easier to ride in the summer as the ground can be waterlogged in winter, making it very hard to ride in places. I found this out for myself the hard way one wet January.

Chobham Common has also had connections with the military. It was used to practise trench warfare during World War I; to identify safe ways of detonating landmines during World War II; and, during the Victorian era, it was used as an army training camp. Queen Victoria visited the camp in 1853 and there is a ❷ **memorial** to this event which you can go to see, not far from the road. So, still on the B383 and 1.4km from the railway bridge, on your left you will see an orange sign for the **Monument Car**

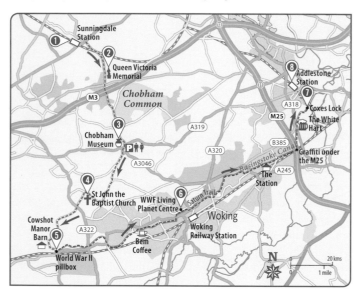

THE TREACLE MINES OF CHOBHAM COMMON

A local legend tells of a mine full of treacle on Chobham Common. The story goes that troops stationed on the Common buried their stores of treacle in the ground and then forgot about them when they moved on. When someone was digging in the ground, they burst the containers and the black liquid spilled forth. How the treacle got there depends on who is telling the tale. It was either British soldiers camped on the Common during the Victorian era or Canadian troops going home after the end of World War I. This apocryphal story is most probably simply a fine example of British humour. Chobham is not the only location of supposed treacle mines in the UK, as it shares this distinction with Tadley in Hampshire, Sabden in Lancashire and Worthing in Sussex, to name but three.

↑ Chobham Common (Robin Castle/S)

Park. It is easy to ride past this sign without seeing it (which is exactly what I did the first time I completed this ride). A quick stop-off here and a walk along the footpath will bring you to the aforementioned memorial (/// unless.client.spoon). From here, you will have a great view of the Common which has been used in numerous films – even doubling up for the Wild West in *Carry On Cowboy*!

Just over 500m after the Monument Car Park is a roundabout. Take the second exit. It is still the B383, but it is now called Windsor Road. 1.75km after the roundabout, you will see the first buildings indicating that you are on the outskirts of **Chobham** village. These include a **16th-century farmhouse** which has now been converted into a restaurant (called The Cloche Hat). This building is quite distinctive with its whitewashed walls, dark timbers, and the fact that the windows on the top floor do not line up. You'll see what I mean when you cycle past.

A further 1.3km on from this point is the main commercial area of Chobham village. You will know that you have arrived because you will see a full-scale model of a horse on your left outside an equestrian shop. He is known locally as Kev, but no-one seems to know why. The road also changes name at this point and becomes High Street (A319). Just along from the equestrian shop and on the same side of the road is Chobham's **war memorial**, as well as a small **cannon** which was placed here as another way of commemorating Queen Victoria and her 1853 visit.

Turn left at the mini roundabout and proceed down High Street (now the A3046). A slight detour, taking a right turn, will take you to the ❸ **Chobham Museum** on your right. It's well worth a visit, even though the building looks like it was once a public toilet. That, in fact, is exactly what it used to be in a previous life.

The High Street is quite narrow for an A-road, but traffic does move slowly down it. What is noticeable about the shops is the lack of chains: most of the businesses are independent traders. On your left, you will see the **St Lawrence Church**, some parts of which date back to 1080. You won't see any gravestones in the churchyard as it is no longer consecrated ground. The bodies of those once buried here are still under the surface, even though the grave markers are long gone, with some

having even been used as paving stones. The church itself is open most days, and I recommend having a chat with the friendly vicar if you get an opportunity. Buried here is Thomas Heath, who was the last Roman Catholic Archbishop of York (1555–59) and Lord Chancellor to Mary I (1556–58).

At the end of High Street, turn right on to Castle Grove Road. Stay on this road for 2.55km. The road changes name twice. First, it is known as Guildford Road and then Chobham Road, before you need to turn right on to Warbury Lane. Just before Warbury Lane is a left turn into Barrs Lane. If you are interested in railways, specifically miniature ones, then pay a visit to **Mizens Railway**. Check the website for opening times as they do not open all year round (⌀ wokingminiaturerailwaysociety.com).

Warbury Lane is a lovely road to cycle as it is surrounded by trees and hedges for almost its entire length. The road becomes slightly wider when you see the sign for **Bisley** village. The road is now known as Church Lane and that is because on your left is ❹ **St John the Baptist Church**. It is quite easy to miss as it is behind the houses and not well signposted. To visit the church, you need to go through a gate in between two houses on your left with a signpost on your right which says 'Bisley Church'.

↑ Chobham cricket field (Robin Castle/S)

This Grade II-listed church goes back to the 13th century, although most of the building dates from the late 1800s, which is when restoration took place. Inside the church itself is a rather fine history, including the story of Rev. John Gwyon who served the parish for 33 years. He was a well-known eccentric who left a trust for the poor boys of Farnham so they could be provided with knickers. 'Knickers' in this case, it should be pointed out, refers to garments similar to the plus fours worn by golfers, and not ladies' underwear.

If you walk through the church grounds, you can pass through the gate and take the footpath until you reach the **Holy Well of St John the Baptist**. The well was most probably a source of water for church baptisms; today, it is topped by a small brick structure with a pipe attached, allowing the water to flow out of it.

Returning to the road, turn left and continue along Church Lane until turning left on to Clews Lane. Turn left at the next junction to continue along Clews Lane, at the end of which is a major junction. This is the Guildford Road (A322). Turn left and then immediately right to enter Queens Road. This junction also has pedestrian crossings.

Continue along Queens Road for 2.58km. You may well hear a regular cracking noise as you cycle through this area. This is the sound of gunfire: you are passing the **National Shooting Centre** at Bisley. Shooting events for the 1908 Olympics and 2002 Commonwealth Games were held here.

As you cycle along this tree-lined road, you will come to Pirbright Bridge, which crosses the **Basingstoke Canal**. The towpath starts just before the bridge, and you need to turn left on to it. You will follow the canal for 13km. You will also be travelling downhill pretty much the whole way, but be mindful as dog walkers, hikers, runners and other cyclists could also be using this path. You also need to be careful when going under the bridges as there are some blind corners. You can see when these are coming up by a sign on the bridge asking cyclists to dismount. Also be wary when going under bridges in case other cyclists are joining the towpath from the left.

The towpath is easy to follow and in good condition but there are some tight turns; during the winter months, it can be covered in a thin layer of mud. You are following the **Basingstoke Canal Towpath/Saturn Trail** as you ride along the canal towards Woking. Woking Borough Council designated several routes in the area for cycling and named them after planets and moons in the solar system. More information about the Planet Trails can be found at ⊘ wokingtrails.637pixels.com.

Meanwhile, our route is still at the beginning of the towpath section. As you join the towpath, you will see a concrete structure behind an information board. This is a ❺ **World War II pillbox**, like the one you passed in Eashing (Ride 3, page 43), built when the British were preparing defensive lines in case of a German invasion.

After 1.58km, you will reach Lock 12. The canal path stops here and you must cross the road. If you cross straight over here, there are a set of steps back on to the canal. However, if you turn left and cross the road at the 'Welcome to Knaphill' sign, you will be back on the Saturn Trail and you will not need to carry your bike down the steps.

At the next bridge, the path deviates slightly from the canal, and you will come to Hermitage Road (A324). Turn right on to the road and cross the bridge. Once you are over the bridge, turn left, go down the slope and you are back on the towpath. There is a blind corner to your right as you come down the slope so be careful as you descend. The towpath is on the southern side of the canal, with the northern side taken up by private houses.

Once again, the path ascends at a bridge. This is **Kiln Bridge**, and you are now in **St John's** village. Turn left and cross over the bridge, before turning right, joining the towpath once more and passing by Lock 11. Once you are 2km on from St John's, you will see some skyscrapers protruding over the treeline. Going under one of the few modern bridges on this route, you are now in Woking town centre. On your right you will see the **New Victoria Theatre** and, on your left, hidden by the trees, is the ❻ **WWF Living Planet Centre**. A tour of the building can be booked in advance through their website (⊘ wwf.org.uk).

The path soon ascends once again, and you need to turn right at the top and cross over to the southern bank once more. As you go up the slope, you will see the rather impressive **The Lightbox** building, which houses an art gallery and museum. You need to cross the Chobham Road (A3046) to rejoin the towpath. This road can be busy but there is a pedestrian crossing on your right.

A further 1.87km after The Lightbox, you will see an interesting piece of black machinery, which dates to the time when this was a working canal. It once had a wooden jib (long since rotted away) which was used to unload coils of wire for a nail factory that was once on this part of the canal. After going under the bridge, look over to the other side of the canal where you will see the **Muslim Burial Ground and Peace Garden**, which is the final resting place for Muslim soldiers who fought for Britain in both world wars.

When you see the sign for Woodham Flight, there is a tight left turn coming up as you go under the bridge. After Lock 1, you will see a concrete bridge looming out from behind the trees. This is the M25 and the end of the Basingstoke Canal. You will need to walk across the footbridge as it has been designed in such a way as to be virtually impossible to ride across. The stretch of water under the bridge is the **River Wey**. Turning left at the bottom of the footbridge, you are now cycling under the M25 and the pillars holding the road aloft are covered in some spectacular graffiti. This path is not shown on komoot but it is easy to navigate as it is as wide as the motorway above it. You will be following the Wey for 2.3km.

After riding along the Wey for 1km, you will reach **New Haw Lock** and the beautiful lock-keeper's cottage. You need to walk up a small staircase and cross over Byfleet Road (A318). Following the path along the River Wey once more, this is the most muddy and least looked-after stretch of the journey.

As you follow the path, a small lake appears on your left and ahead of you is an impressive building. You are now at ❼ **Coxes Lock**. The lake is the **Mill Pond**, and the building is the mill, which dates from the late 1700s and produced both steel and flour at various times during its lifetime. Grain was brought from the Royal Docks in London and along the Wey to the mills until the 1960s. The lock itself dates from the mid-1600s and is the deepest unmanned lock on the river. The building itself has been converted into residential properties.

Cross over the lock, then a bridge, and keep going until you reach Bourneside Road. Follow this road until you reach a roundabout. Turn right on to Corrie Road and follow it to the end. Turn right on to Station Road (B3121). You will soon come to ❽ **Addlestone Station** and the conclusion of this ride.

THE ESSENTIALS

GETTING THERE By train, Sunningdale is a 48-minute journey from London Waterloo. By car, Sunningdale is 9.5km from Junction 13 of the M25 and then along the A30. Alternatively, it is 7km from Junction 3 of the M3, along the A322 and then the A30. Addlestone is not on the same railway line as Sunningdale, but you can get back to that station by changing at Virginia Water Station.

FACILITIES AND FURTHER INFORMATION There are public toilets in Chobham High Street car park. **Chobham Museum**'s website (⌖ museum.chobham.org) is a mine of information about the village and surrounding area.

WHERE TO EAT

Basil & Blue, 88 High St, Chobham, GU24 8LZ. Located before the High St in Chobham, just behind the Queen Victoria cannon. Hot drinks, light bites, cakes and bakes as well as iced drinks in the summer. There is plenty of outdoor seating for the cyclist in need of a break. **£**

Bem Coffee, 9 St Johns Rd, St John's, Woking, GU21 7SE; ☎ 01483 726446; ⌖ bemcoffee. co.uk. Located a few metres from Kiln Bridge, this is a perfect stop off for a cyclist. Serves light bites, hot drinks, milkshakes and a selection of fruit smoothies. **£**

The White Hart, New Haw Rd, Addlestone, KT15 2DS; ☎ 01932 842927; ⌖ thewhitehartnewhaw.co.uk. You may well want something more substantial after that ride, while sitting by the banks of the River Wey in an award-winning garden. The White Hart has a good deal of choice ranging from light bites to full meals. It is advisable to ring ahead to check the opening hours as I have been caught out turning up a bit late. **£–££**

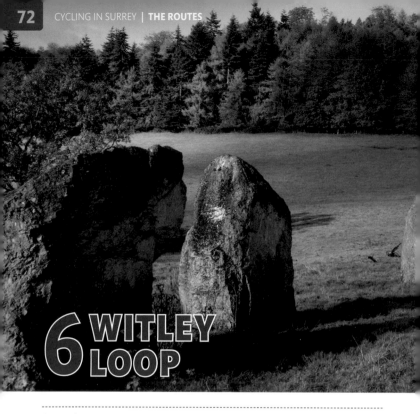

6 WITLEY LOOP

START/FINISH	Witley Railway Station
DISTANCE/TIME	22.2km/2hrs (extension: 6.3km, 45mins; alt. route: 2km, 10mins)
DIFFICULTY/TERRAIN	② An undulating ride following on- and off-road routes; you will cross some A-roads and ride along B-roads and country lanes
SCENIC RATING	⑧ Passing through villages and peaceful countryside, seeing historic churches and inns
SUITABLE FOR	MTB, gravel, hybrid or road bike
CYCLE ROUTE	Surrey Cycleway
MAPS	OS Explorer OL33 and OL34 (1:25 000)
KOMOOT REF	891009274

↑ Hascombe Stone Circle (Alan Whitehead/S)

One of the few rides in this book that can be completed on a road bike, this route takes in some beautiful country roads, quiet villages, historic churches, and an 18th-century labourer's cottage. If your timing is right, you can also visit some spectacular gardens. A road bike is not recommended, however, should you decide to follow the alternative route described below.

THE ROUTE

As you come out of ❶ **Witley Railway Station**, take a left on to Robin Way. Turn right on to Combe Lane and then left on New Road. Turn right on to Petworth Road (A283) and then turn immediately left on to Lane End, following the sign to Hambledon Village Shop. Once you pass the houses, the road becomes lined with trees. Turn right at the road sign 'The Cricket

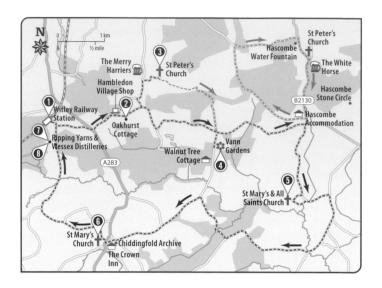

Green leading to Vann Lane'. As you come out of the trees, you will see a pond on your left and next to that is **Hambledon Village Shop**, which is not just a shop but a Post Office and café as well (see below).

Passing by the shop, you will see Hambledon Cricket Club's green on your right. As you come towards the end of the green, you will see a sign for ❷ **Oakhurst Cottage**, an 19th-century labourer's cottage now maintained by the National Trust (limited opening from April to October with pre-booking required via ⌖ nationaltrust.org.uk). Continue along Vann Lane and, 500m after the Hambledon Village Shop, turn left on to Woodlands Road, which is part of the Surrey Cycleway. At the end of the road, turn right on to Hambledon Road where the signpost directs you towards Busbridge and Godalming. Follow the road until you reach the right turn into Church Lane, or carry straight on for 100m for the rather fabulous **The Merry Harriers** pub (see *Accommodation*, page 221). As Church Lane gently ascends, after 300m you will see ❸ **St Peter's Church** on your left. The original church is believed to have been built in the 1200s and was rebuilt during the Victorian era. There are two great yew trees in the churchyard and the larger of the two has been dated to around the 8th century. If you follow Church Lane to the end of the churchyard and look right, you will see an old lime kiln. Lime has been used for centuries to make mortar, which in turn was used to bind building materials such as bricks and stone together. The sign above the kiln says that it was in use until the 10th century, but I would take that dating with a pinch of salt. Take a right just before the lime kiln to follow the alternative route (see below).

Retrace your steps, going back the way you came along the Surrey Cycleway. When you come to the end of Woodlands Road, turn left to pick up on Vann Lane where you left off. Continue for 2km to a point where the road turns right. Ahead of you is a signpost for Pockford and Chiddingfold. Continue along the road for 300m and on your left you will see a stunning 16th-century house by the name of ❹ **Vann** (🔗 vanngarden. co.uk). It is surrounded by five acres of charming gardens that can be visited at certain times of the year. To return to the route, turn right out of Vann, retracing your steps back along Vann Lane. Take the next

↑ Oakhurst Cottage in Hambledon (Ross Hamilton)

right which takes you into **Burgate Farm** where you will leave the Surrey Cycleway. Even though the sign says 'Private Road', you are permitted to cycle here. For the next 2km, you will traverse farmland which, even on a dull day, is quite lovely. Near the end of this stretch, you will pass through a pair of gates and see a set of small-gauge railway tracks embedded in the road. I have been unable to ascertain what this railway was used for, whether it is still in use, or how long it has been here.

At the T-junction, turn right on to Hook House Lane (if you want to try the extension, don't turn right but continue to the main road; see below). Follow the road for 1.6km before turning right on to Church Road. As the road takes a sharp left, look to your right where you will see ❺ **St Mary's and All Saints Church**, which dates to the 13th century. Walk through the gateway and you will see a yew tree which is so old that the trunk is now hollow. This is a natural process and does not mean the tree has died. Entering the church you will see a tapestry, made by parishioners for the Millennium in 2000, using similar colours to those found in the west window. The pews are thought to be some of the oldest in England and also date back to the 13th century. If you wish to explore further, turn right out of the churchyard and make your way down the hill to what

is now called the **Holy Well**. How long this has been considered holy is debatable, because on Ordinance Survey maps from the 1800s it is listed as a tank. The shrine above the well is dedicated to the Virgin Mary and the water within, which is said to be high in chlorine, has been used for baptisms down the years. I did not notice any signs advising against drinking it but I must say it did not look appealing.

Make your way back up the footpath and turn right on to Church Road once more. At the junction,

↑ The Holy Well in Dunsfold (Ross Hamilton)

turn right on to Shoppe Hill. Follow this to Dunsfold Common Road, where you need to turn right once again. You are now entering the village of **Dunsfold**. Fans of the BBC TV programme *Top Gear* might recognise the name 'Dunsfold Aerodrome', as the show's test track is not far from here. As you ride down Dunsfold Common Road, the buildings on your right have been erected behind what used to be a more substantial common. Look out on your left for **Winn Hall**, which was built between 1914 and 1916 by the Underwoods, who were also responsible for constructing several other local buildings designed by the architect Edwin Lutyens (see Ride 3, page 49). Although Winn Hall was not a Lutyens design, those who know his work will recognise certain features betraying his influence. On your right is The Sun Inn and on your left is the Dunsfold war memorial. You are now back on the Surrey Cycleway. For the next 2.8km the road changes its name from Dunsfold Common Road to Wrotham Hill to Chiddingfold Road to High Street Green.

Turn right into White Beech Lane; when you get to the end of this road, turn left and on to a more southerly stretch of Vann Lane. After 1.3km, the road changes its name to Pockford Road. At the junction, turn right and then take an almost immediate left on to The Green. You are now in the village of **Chiddingfold**, once home to a thriving glass-manufacturing industry. Both Henry III and Edward II purchased glass in Chiddingfold for the decoration of Westminster Abbey and St George's Chapel at Windsor Castle, respectively. On The Green, you will pass **Elliott's Coffee Shop** and **The Chiddingfold Archive** (see below). On the corner of The Green, you will see the historic **The Crown Inn** to your left (see *Accommodation*, page 221) and ahead of you is ❻ **St Mary's Church**. This building can be dated to the 13th century, even though only the chancel can claim to be so old; the rest dates to the Victorian era. As you walk through the porch, look behind the font: the window there bears witness to the village's past. It is dedicated to the local glass-makers and was constructed in 1916 from glass excavated from the remains of local glasshouses.

Cross over Petworth Road (A283) and head up Coxcombe Lane. Take a left on to Ridgley Road which changes its name to Combe Lane after 800m.

RED TELEPHONE BOXES

Before mobiles became an almost essential part of daily life, if you wanted to make a phone call on the move you had to use a public telephone. The first dedicated phone box was introduced in the UK in 1921 – the imaginatively titled Kiosk Number 1 (shortened to K1). There would be a further four attempts at phone boxes and they were mostly painted red so that they would be easy to see. The red telephone box has since become something of a British icon, with one appearing on the cover of records by artists such as David Bowie and One Direction and featuring prominently in films such as the original version of *The Ladykillers*. However, with the rise of mobile phones, the telephone boxes' days were numbered. All the same, you will see quite a few K6s – the most famous design – while riding around Surrey. Some of them still have their phones inside, but others have been adapted for other uses. On my travels, I have seen them house defibrillators (pages 26, 32 and 199), displays about a village's history (pages 34 and 165), a community noticeboard (page 151), a tool station (page 154) and a miniature art gallery (page 26).

↑ Left to right: Phone boxes used as an art gallery in Frensham (Ride 1) and a village history kiosk in Leigh (Ride 16) (Ross Hamilton)

You will soon pass a road sign showing that Witley Railway Station is only 1½ miles away. You will also be leaving the Surrey Cycleway here. Before you reach Witley Station, though, keep an eye out to your left – at 1.5km after the road sign to the station – for a sign to Cooper's Place. This is a trading estate and home to the ❼ **Wessex Distillery** (⌂ wessexdistillery. com) and the ❽ **Ripping Yarns Distillery** (⌂ rippingyarnsdistillery.com). Both produce an award-winning product (gin and rum, respectively) and are well worth a stop-off. The next left turn is Station Approach, which will take you to Witley Railway Station and the end of this ride.

ALTERNATIVE ROUTE: GREENSAND WAY

This alternative route is designed for those who like their off-road riding and something a bit more challenging. You need to take the right turn just before the lime kiln and head along **Greensand Way** (Bridleway 185) for just under 1km. This can be quite muddy but, even after several days' rain (which is what we'd had before I travelled down it for the first time), it is still navigable. Just be prepared to get covered in mud, especially if you do not have any mudguards (like my travelling companion). At the junction, turn right on to Bridleway 190, also part of Greensand Way. When you see some houses on your right, you will be joining Upper Vann Lane where the road surface improves. When you come to the junction, turn left on to Vann Lane, rejoining our main route.

EXTENSION: HASCOMBE VILLAGE

Instead of turning right on to Hook House Lane, turn left on to Godalming Road (B2130) and then a sharp left on to Markwick Lane. There are very few buildings along this road and on your right as you ride is **Holloways Heath**. You will also be riding next to **Breakneck Hill** but don't let the name put you off! After riding this lovely stretch of road for 2.5km, turn right on to Mare Lane. This is an equally enjoyable stretch of road, but it is quite narrow so look out for oncoming vehicles. After 1.4km, you will reach **Hascombe** village, known for its nearby stone circle. However, this was not built by our prehistoric ancestors but by modern-day druids in the late 1990s. Turn right on to The Street (B2130) and look to your

right for **Hascombe Spring Fountain**, which was built by local resident Edward Rowcliffe in 1877 in memory of his brother. The legend above the fountain welcomes you to take the water freely, but another, more recent sign says that the water is untested, so you drink it at your own risk. As with the Holy Well in Dunsfold, I chose not to partake.

Continue along the B2130 until you come to **The White Horse** pub. Take a left before the pub and pay a visit to **St Peter's Church**. Like St Peter's in Hambledon, this church was originally built in the 1200s but many features now date to the Victorian era. The artwork is spectacular and shows images from the life of the saint, including his catch of 153 fish when he first encountered Jesus, which are depicted along the walls. Ride back to The White Horse and, if you're not stopping for something to eat or drink, turn left on to The Street. It soon changes its name to Godalming Road. After 1.4km turn right on to Hook House Lane and follow it round to the left. You've now rejoined the main route and are heading towards Dunsfold.

↑ The decorated interior of the Church of St Peter in Hascombe (AndyScott/WC)

THE ESSENTIALS

GETTING THERE By train, the journey from London Waterloo is 59 minutes. By car, Witley Railway Station is 3km from Milford via the A283. There is a pay-and-display car park next to the station.

FACILITIES AND FURTHER INFORMATION The Hambledon Village Shop has a toilet around the back of the main building, but it is only available when the café is open. Pop along to the **Chiddingfold Archive** (⊘ thechiddingfoldarchive.org.uk) if you want to learn more about Chiddingfold's history.

WHERE TO EAT

Hambledon Village Shop, The Cricket Green, Hambledon, GU8 4HF; ⊘ 01428 682176; ⊘ hambledonvillageshop.co.uk. Light bites as well as a selection of cold and hot drinks are available. There is also a wide selection of delicious cakes. Outdoor seating only. **£**

The Sun Inn, Sun Inn Rd, The Common, Dunsfold, GU8 4LE; ⊘ 01483 200242; ⊘ suninndunsfold.co.uk. Set back from the road, this inn dates back some 400 years. Food, which includes light bites and main meals, is served daily (except Mon). Local beers are available from Dunsfold's own Crafty Brewing. **£–££**

Elliott's Coffee Shop, The Green, Chiddingfold, GU8 4TU; ⊘ 07539 312711; ⊘ elliottscoffeeshop.com. Located on Chiddingfold Green, this is a lovely place to relax during your ride, especially if the weather is nice enough to sit outside. The menu consists of light bites and some lovely cakes. I can highly recommend the caramel milkshake. The kitchen is not open on a Sunday. **£**

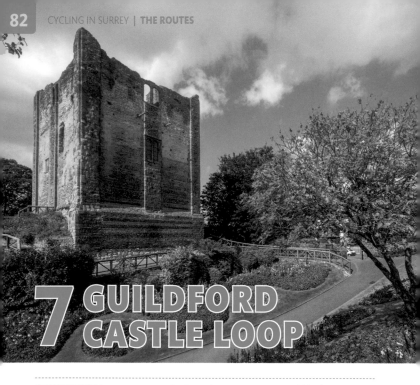

7 GUILDFORD CASTLE LOOP

START/FINISH	Castle Arch, Quarry Street, Guildford
DISTANCE/TIME	14.5km/1½hrs (2 extensions; 1: 2.8km, 30mins; 2: 1.5km round trip, 15mins; alt. route: 2.2km, 20mins)
DIFFICULTY/TERRAIN	① Flat for most of the ride following B-roads, paths and an abandoned railway; hilly on the latter stages
SCENIC RATING	© Country roads, abandoned railway, woodland and a common
SUITABLE FOR	MTB, gravel or sturdy hybrid (with off-road tyres)
CYCLE ROUTE	NCN22
MAPS	OS Explorer 145 (1:25 000)
KOMOOT REF	879552155

↑ Guildford Castle (Gillian Pullinger/S)

Taking in one of Surrey's ten castles, you will follow the only defunct railway in this county closed due to the 1963 Beeching Report. You will pass through charming villages and see venerable churches and captivating countryside. This ride includes two extensions and an alternative route which takes in more of the history of this area.

THE ROUTE

You start this ride at the ❶ **Castle Arch**, which is right next to the Guildford Museum. Turn left and head down Quarry Street, so named as chalk was once quarried in this area. At the traffic lights, go straight across Millbrook (A281) and on to the pavement, turning left on to NCN22. The pavement here is a cycle path. Pass by The Weyside pub and continue along the cycle track until the path ends. Here, you need to turn right, and you will be entering **Shalford Park**, following Dagley Lane.

You will soon arrive at Shalford Park car park. Continue along the track and you will come to a signpost next to some black and yellow bollards. If you wish to take the alternative route (see below), turn right at this signpost. The cycle lane bears to the right and then left. You will pass over a small bridge that crosses the **River Tillingbourne**. Continue along the path until you reach the car park for the Shalford Water Treatment Plant. To the left is ❷ **St Mary's Church, Shalford**. Mentioned in the Domesday Book, this is the fourth church to occupy this site. Inside the chancel, you will find a brass dating back to 1509, dedicated to the memory of a Roger Elyot, a collector of rents for Henry VIII. This is the oldest monument in the church. Turn right as you walk in for a list of all the known vicars of Shalford from 1199, with a notes section giving information about their life and times – quite an interesting read.

NCN22 continues through the car park and turns into a dirt track once you have passed the metal fence on your right. This can be muddy, and you will have to navigate some wooden steps as the path climbs upwards. At the top, turn right. Follow the paved track for 500m and continue straight on after you cross the railway bridge. The route is not so well paved here, and the pot-holes can be full of water. Once you have passed through the park, turn left and then immediately right on to Broadford Road (A248). You will soon come to a bridge, which is quite narrow, and it is advisable to cross only if no traffic is coming the other way, or to walk across on the footpath to your right. As soon as you have crossed the bridge, join the cycle lane that runs parallel to the road on the right-hand side. Follow this lane for 480m, turn left under the bridge and you'll see a National Trust sign to your left: this is the route you will need to follow. You are now on what was once the **Cranleigh Railway** line. See Ride 8 (page 96) for more information on this now abandoned line.

This path also follows the route once occupied by the **Wey & Arun Canal**. Although most of it was sold off following closure in the late 1800s

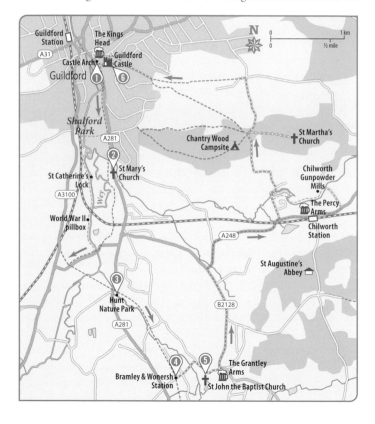

due to competition from the railway, stretches of the canal network have been restored (see box, page 87). The trail is straight and flat but you can get muddy riding along here. You will need to cross the Horsham Road (A281); although it has a traffic island, it can be busy so please be careful.

On the other side of the road is the ❸ **Hunt Nature Park**. The Wey & Arun Canal Trust has a visitor centre to your right but it is only open when a volunteer is in attendance. This is an area of great biodiversity, most of which is detailed on the information boards. You can see peacock butterflies and kingfishers here, and, if you are lucky (I was not), red deer.

You pass under a road bridge as the track bears to the left and quickly arrive at the remains of ❹ **Bramley and Wonersh Station**. Both platforms and the level crossing barriers have survived. On the left-hand platform is a potted history of the station and a plaque commemorating those who lost their lives here when the train they were on was bombed and strafed during a World War II air raid.

At the level crossing, turn left on to Station Road and the Surrey Cycleway. Continue along Station Road for 400m until you get to a T-junction. Turn right on to The Street. On your right is ❺ **St John the Baptist Church**. The church is said to date to Anglo-Saxon times but was rebuilt during the Norman era. The interior of the church still has several Norman features and, if you look carefully at the floor in the North Chapel, you can see several encaustic tiles which are believed to be from the Middle Ages. Unusually, the tower has a clock in it.

As you continue along The Street to the village of **Wonersh**, on your right is a low wall and a gatehouse. The gatehouse was once the entrance to Wonersh Mansion, which was built in the 17th century. The Mansion was demolished in 1935, the gatehouse and the wall being all that remain. If you look through the gate, you will see several sculptures depicting local people and their activities during World War II. The gatehouse is now home to a colony of bats.

As The Street bears round to the right, note a sign on the building on your right which says '**The Old House**'. These buildings were once home to the Wonersh wool-weaving industry. Known as kersey or Wonersh Blue, the woollen cloth they produced was sold in western Europe and the Canary Islands. As you turn left, just after the red telephone box there is a small building in the middle of the road junction. Known locally as the 'Pepper Pot', it was built as a bus shelter. It is no longer used as such, possibly down to the fact that it suffered several collisions during its lifetime. You may notice that street lighting is conspicuous by its absence in Wonersh. The local History Society was unable to offer any clue as to why this might be, and there does not seem to be much interest in changing the situation. The one street lamp that was installed, to illuminate a particularly dark section of pavement, has now been partly obscured by a large tree. At the Pepper Pot, turn left on to Wonersh Common (B2128).

Continue along Wonersh Common for 1.4km and then turn right into New Road (A248). Follow New Road for 1.5km and then take a left on to Blacksmith Lane; or, if you are taking Extension 1, continue straight on for the **Chilworth Gunpowder Mills** (see below). Staying on the main route, you will cross the River Tillingbourne once again, and the road becomes Halfpenny Lane. This road continues for 2km and you will be cycling steadily uphill – a 10% gradient at one point. The road is narrow in places but there are lay-bys to allow oncoming traffic to pass.

After 1.3km, you see a sign for St Martha's Hill and its car park. A right turn here will take you to **St Martha's Church** (see Extension 2 below). Follow the road until you see a red post box on your left. Turn left here and go on to Longdown Road. The road bears off to the left but you need to head along the path straight in front of you. Follow the path until it opens on to **Pewley Down**, which was donated to Guildford by the long-gone Friary Brewery in memory of those who perished in World War I. If you look to your left, not only will you see a memorial to this but you will have an incredible view of the area you have just traversed (/// menu. renew.asks).

Follow the dirt track as it bears around to the right and you will eventually come to Pewley Hill. Ride through the bollards and on to the road. At the corner of Semaphore Road, the white building with the octagonal domed roof on your right is **Semaphore House**, which was once part of the signalling system from London to Portsmouth (see Ride 11,

WEY & ARUN CANAL

The Wey & Arun Canal was created to link the River Wey (in Surrey) and the River Arun (in West Sussex) to act as a safe route from the English Channel to London during the Napoleonic Wars. However, the wars were over before the canal was finished. It was used for many years to carry goods such as coal, timber and lime until the railways threatened it, as they did the canal network throughout the country. The ultimate death knell for the Wey & Arun Canal was the Cranleigh Railway (see Ride 8, page 96) in 1865. In 1868, an Act of Parliament approved the canal's closure, which was finalised in 1871. A hundred years later, a group of enthusiasts formed the Wey & Arun Canal Trust (WACT; ⚓ weyarun.org.uk), dedicated to the restoration of its entire 37km. Twenty-eight of the original 49 bridges have been restored or rebuilt, as well as 11 of the 28 lock chambers and two of the three original aqueducts. WACT owns or leases 36% of the course of the canal, which is otherwise owned by several rural landowners, although most of the restored sections and structures can be accessed along parts of its towpath designated as bridleways forming part of the Wey-South Path. For much of the year WACT operates boat trips over 5km of the canal centred on Loxwood, West Sussex.

↑ A lock on the Wey & Arun Canal (Paul Briden/S)

page 127). At this point, you will start to head down a rather steep hill, so be careful – but you do get an excellent view of Guildford here, including the Cathedral. At the T-junction turn left on to South Hill, then take the next right and go down Castle Hill. This is another steep slope, with caution recommended when the road bears around to the right as it's a sharp turn. As you turn right, there are two houses to your right. The first is the one in which Lewis Carroll, author of *Alice in Wonderland*, died (see also Ride 2, page 37). You will see the remains of ❻ **Guildford Castle** directly ahead of you and, as the road bears to the left, you will see Castle Arch once again and you have now reached your destination.

ALTERNATIVE ROUTE:
RIVER WEY AND ST CATHERINE'S LOCK

A bit more challenging than the main route, this is designed for those who like their off-road riding. Not long after you have passed the Shalford Park changing rooms/toilets, you will come to some black and yellow bollards. Turn right here, following the dirt track before entering the trees. The trail comes to a T-junction; turn left and head towards **Ferry Lane Bridge**. Next to the bridge is a wooden memorial commemorating the fact that this land was once part of Shalford House, a now demolished country home. Shalford Park was once monastic land, but it was bought by the local council to protect it from housing development and in order for it to be used for 'public pleasure'. You will need to carry your bike up the steps of the bridge to get to the other side. Once on the opposite bank, turn left. You are at the base of **St Catherine's Hill**. At the top of this hill is **St Catherine's Chapel**, which dates to the 14th century but is now a ruin and closed off to the public. It is well worth a walk up there, though, if you have the time.

The first section of this route, along the River Wey, is undulating, and in places it might be easier (and safer) to walk. The river path is a popular walking route and the river itself is used by paddleboarders, kayakers and the odd canal boat. As you travel along the river, you will see alders, which used to be coppiced and transported down the river to the Chilworth Gunpowder Mills (see Extension 1 below) to be used as charcoal. The water meadows by the riverside are also home to several plants such as sedge, marsh marigold and red campion. Many insects use the rotting wood as their home, which attracts birds such as woodpeckers and treecreepers. You will soon come to **St Catherine's Lock** which, according to the sign, was opened in 1764 and is the shallowest lock on the Wey. Further on, just past the metal railway bridge and up a slope on your right, you will see a **World War II pillbox**. There were a number of these built in Surrey to act as a defensive line to protect London from a potential German invasion. The path eventually slopes upwards, and you will come to Broadford Road (A248). Turn right to rejoin NCN22 and our main route as it heads towards the disused railway.

EXTENSION 1: CHILWORTH GUNPOWDER MILLS

As New Road becomes Dorking Road, continue straight instead of turning left into Blacksmith Lane. As you make your way through **Chilworth** village, look out for **The Percy Arms** on your left and, 500m after passing the pub, turn left at the sign for Longfrey Farm and Longfrey Cottage. Continue down this road until you cross over the River Tillingbourne. Turn left on to a trail, which I recommend you walk along to begin with as the path is very narrow. You will pass by a watercourse as well as a series of ruined buildings. These are the remains of the **Chilworth Gunpowder Mills**. Gunpowder was produced here, on and off, between 1626 and 1920. Information leaflets can be found at the site if you wish to learn more. Apart from the ruins, this area is home to several insect species such as dragonflies and damselflies. If you are lucky, you may see one of the three types of bat that live here, as do hazel dormice. As you continue along the trail and bear to the right, you will see on the other side of the river a pair of wooden snails dedicated to Samantha Western, who, during her short life, loved to play in the stream and hunt for snails. The left-hand snail is in poor condition but has been left as it is to serve as a bug hotel. The trail now bears around to the right. This area is popular with walkers and their dogs, so don't ride too fast. The trail then bears around to the left and you will come to a green gate. Pass through the gate and turn right on to Halfpenny Lane, rejoining the ride.

EXTENSION 2: ST MARTHA'S CHURCH

The current church was rebuilt between 1848 and 1850 as the original 12th-century church – which, it is believed, was built to act as a landmark for pilgrims making their way to either Winchester or Canterbury cathedrals – had fallen into ruin. Turn right off Halfpenny Lane where the car park sign is for St Martha's Hill. Carry on past both the car park (on your left) and 'Private Drive' sign (on your right), until the paved surface reverts to Surrey's infamous sandy soil. The route uphill is 700m long. Once you reach the treeline, the ground becomes less sandy, but the gradient starts to increase. According to the Visit Surrey website, the view from the grounds around this church is so magnificent that, on a clear day, you can see up to seven counties. Although the church is only open Sunday mornings, this extension is worthwhile for the view alone – in my opinion one of the best, if not the best, in Surrey.

↑ Remains of the old boiler house at Chilworth Gunpowder Mills (Alex Manders/S)

THE ESSENTIALS

GETTING THERE By train, the closest station is Guildford; from London Waterloo it takes about 40 minutes on the fast train. By car, Millbrook Car Park is a couple of minutes' walk away from Castle Arch and, if you do drive, you could start here as you will pass through the arch on your way back.

FACILITIES There are public toilets in Shalford Park, Guildford.

WHERE TO EAT

The Grantley Arms, The Street, Wonersh, GU5 0PE; ✆ 01483 893351; ♘ thegrantleyarms. co.uk. This historic pub uses the village's old bakery as part of its dining area. It has a selection of seasonal menus featuring light bites as well as three-course meals. **££**

The Percy Arms, 75 Dorking Rd, Chilworth, GU4 8NP; ✆ 01483 561765; ♘ thepercyarms. net. An extensive menu of full meals and lighter bites such as sandwiches is available, mixing British and African flavours. Booking in advance is advisable. **££**

The Kings Head, Quarry St, Guildford, GU1 3XQ; ✆ 01483 575004; ♘ thekingsheadpub. co.uk. This pub is said to be the oldest in Guildford, as well as the most haunted. Full meals and light bites are available as well as vegan options. **£–££**

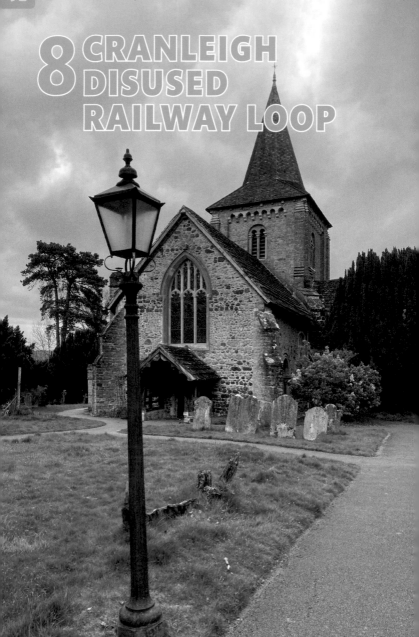

8 CRANLEIGH DISUSED RAILWAY LOOP

START/FINISH	Chilworth Railway Station
DISTANCE/TIME	38.2km/3½hrs
DIFFICULTY/TERRAIN	② A steady climb at the beginning of the ride but mostly downhill with some off-road sections; you cross some A-roads, and ride along B-roads and country lanes
SCENIC RATING	⑧ A common, woodland and a ride along a disused railway as well as country roads
SUITABLE FOR	MTB, gravel or sturdy hybrid (with off-road tyres)
CYCLE ROUTE	Surrey Cycleway, NCN22, NCN223
MAPS	OS Explorer 145 and OL34 (1:25 000)
KOMOOT REF	888664119

This is one of the longest and most scenic rides in the book. You ride over Blackheath Common making your way through the Surrey Hills. There are several historic and unique churches to see on this ride, and you will be travelling along a disused railway line. Look closely and you will also find another of Surrey's lost castles. There are several single-track roads and there is high chance of getting muddy.

THE ROUTE

Come out of ❶ **Chilworth Railway Station** and head south along Sampleoak Lane for 1km. The road climbs gently uphill and, on your left, there is a sign for ❷ **St Augustine's Abbey** (⌂ chilworthbenedictines. com). If you would like to pay this living monastery a visit, keep riding until the next right turning which is the main entrance. Other rides (Rides 2, page 30, and 9, page 102) in this book visit the ruins of several monasteries but this is a functioning one and there aren't many of those in Surrey. The church building is open every day of the year and it is definitely worth a visit. The monks are welcoming to all visitors, regardless of faith or lack thereof. You can even stay here if you so wish (see *Accommodation*, page 224). To leave, use the same entrance you came through, rather than the other exit (it will save you riding up the slope you have already ridden).

← Church of St Peter and St Paul in Ewhurst (Ross Hamilton)

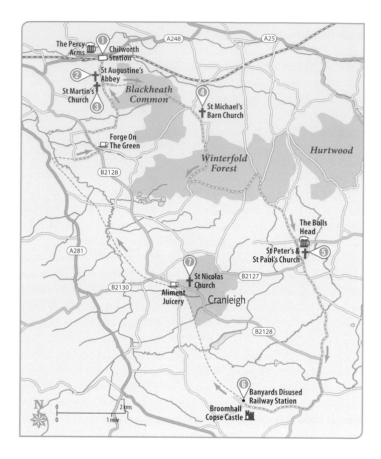

Continue along the road; there is a sign for **Blackheath** village. This is not to be confused with the arguably more famous Blackheath in London, and it contains some rather unusual landmarks, one of which is the sign at the crossroads. It points in three directions with the destinations being 'This Way', 'That Way' and 'Somewhere Else'. No-one is quite sure who placed the original sign here, but local legend places the blame on a Mr Saunders who ran The Volunteer Arms, a pub that once stood near

this location but is now a private residence. He is alleged to have taken drunken visitors from his pub to this crossroads at closing time and asked them if they were going 'this way, that way or somewhere else'. Another unusual landmark is ❸ **St Martin's Church**. Turn right at the crossroads, on to Blackheath Lane, and the church is on your left. As far as churches in Surrey go, this is a unique-looking building, its design inspired by Italian wayside chapels. The interior walls of this Grade II-listed building have murals painted by American artist Anna Lea Merritt.

Head back to the crossroads and go straight across, continuing along Blackheath Lane. Once you pass through the car park, you will be on **Blackheath Common**. This common is classed as heathland and is a Site of Special Scientific Interest (SSSI). It is managed by the local council to prevent invasive species from destroying this now threatened habitat. Fifty-five species of spiders have been recorded here, including the rare lynx spider. Look out for sand lizards as you ride along the paths. Queen Victoria visited Blackheath Common in 1864 to review the local troops, which is where the pub (now closed down) got its name.

Blackheath Common has numerous paths to go exploring on, but be warned: some of them are very sandy and difficult to ride. As you make your way along the track, look left for a wooden fence. Head towards this and down the slope but do take care as there are tree roots sticking out of the ground making this section a little bumpy. Follow this route for 2.3km. When you reach the T-junction, turn left on to August Lane and note a sign for **Farley Green**. Look out for the pond on the green which is on your right. Rumour has it that the pond is linked to a Roman temple, the remains of which have been uncovered on nearby Farley Heath. It is believed that this pond was once the latrine pit for the temple. At the end of the green, turn right on to Shophouse Lane.

↑ The 'This Way That Way' sign in Blackheath (Ross Hamilton)

THE CRANLEIGH LINE

Now known by the name of the largest settlement on the route, this line was officially known as the Horsham & Guildford District Railway. However, better known as the Cranleigh line, it entered service in October 1865. Its purpose was to connect, as its official name implies, the stations of Horsham and Guildford. This it did, although the areas through which it ran were not highly populated. The line had a single track, with passing points built at Baynards, Cranleigh and Bramley & Wonersh stations. This meant that only 14 trains were able to travel on it per day, seven in each direction. Neither passenger numbers nor freight were sufficient in quantity, and when the railways were nationalised in 1948, lines that were losing money faced threat of closure. The Cranleigh line survived the initial wave of closures, but then came Richard Beeching. He was brought in by the government of the day to help streamline a rail network that was losing £300,000 a day: a lot of money in 1961. His report, *The Reshaping of British Railways*, identified the under-used lines and, by the end of the 1960s, around 6,000 miles of tracks had been closed, including numerous stations, which meant job losses too. The Cranleigh line was among them, and it has the unfortunate distinction of being the only route in Surrey to be closed by Beeching. With its track bed removed, the line became one of many Beeching victims repurposed as part of the National Cycle Network. Studies have been conducted into the possibility of reopening the line between Guildford and Cranleigh, but it remains closed.

Farley Green hosts the second 'unique' church on this ride. ❹ **St Michael's** was a 19th-century barn belonging to the Courtenay-Wells family. When Mr Courtenay-Wells died in 1929, his widow decided that the building should be converted into a church in her husband's memory. This is the only public building in Farley Green. If you look above the door, you will see the church bell. There was a ban on church bells being rung in World War II, as they were only to be used to warn of invasion. Panic broke out in the hamlet during the war when the St Michael's bell began to ring. It turned out that a cow had caught herself on the bell rope and set the bell ringing as she tried to escape.

After you pass the church, you will be cycling uphill for the next 4.5km. Follow Shophouse Lane until you reach its end, then turn right at the post box and on to Row Lane. You will notice that the sides of the roads have a lot more trees along them. This is because you are now riding through **Winterfold Forest** and, after that, **Hurtwood**. Several films have been shot here, including *Beauty and the Beast* starring Emma Watson, and the Tom Cruise version of *The Mummy*. After 1.7km on Row Lane, turn left on to Winterfold Heath Road. You will be on this road for another 1.7km. When you reach the T-junction, turn left on to Barhatch Road. You will be pleased to know that it is mostly downhill from now on.

Continue along this road until you reach the next T-junction and then turn right on to Hound House Road. The road soon becomes Pitch Hill. The peak of this hill is near the left turn on to Moon Hall Road and is the seventh highest peak in the Surrey Hills at 259m. You can pick up a lot of speed coming down Pitch Hill: be careful when this road turns into Shere Road – the road surface is not very good as the route bears to the right, so I recommend reducing your speed before you get to this point. As the road continues, you will be riding downhill so ensure that you reduce your speed once more as you pass the signs for **Ewhurst** village before coming to a mini roundabout.

Continue straight on at the mini roundabout on to The Street (B2127) and, after 400m, look to your left to see the Ewhurst **war memorial**. Just behind this is ❺ **St Peter's and St Paul's Church**. The foundation date of the church is uncertain, but it was here in 1223 when the earliest known rector is mentioned. It is now a Grade I-listed building. The churchyard contains a leaping board which has begun to rot away. Look out for the gravestone of John Worsfold which has a carving of Father Time on it and a broken headstone, said to have been damaged when the church tower collapsed in 1837. This is easy to disprove because the date on the gravestone shows that the person buried within died in 1850. Why it is split remains a mystery. The church has been restored many times over the centuries and has been awarded a John Betjeman Award for the repairs to the roof.

As The Street bears around to the right, continue straight ahead on to The Green and follow this road for 1.25km, at which point **Larkfield Pond** is on your left. This is a dew pond with most of its water coming from rainfall, and been designed as a home for frogs, newts and mayflies, as well as several species of plant. Turn right on to Somersbury Lane and follow it for 2.4km. At the T-junction, turn left on to the B2128 following the sign to Rudgwick. You will be on this road for the next 4km, passing through the hamlets of **Ellen's Green** and **Cox Green**. When you pass the road sign for Furzen Lane (in Ellen's Green), you will then be riding along the Surrey Cycleway. Pass through Cox Green, exiting along Cox Green Road.

As you near the 4km mark, cross over a bridge and there is a rather impressive house on your right. To your left is **Broomhall Copse** which is the location of one of Surrey's lost castles. Known by a few names including Cranleigh, Rudgwick and Lynwick, it is also the most difficult to find because komoot doesn't have a route that will take you to it. If you wish to do a bit of exploring, turn left straight after you cross the bridge on Cox Green Road, and continue along NCN223. The location is near /// veered.surcharge.gravy. There is not a lot to see as it is completely overgrown but, if you look closely, you may see the defensive dry ditch that still survives around the site.

When you see the red telephone box ahead of you, turn right on to Station Road. As the wall on your left finishes, a one-storey red-brick building appears. This used to be ❻ **Baynards Railway Station**, a station on the Cranleigh line which linked Guildford and Horsham, before it was closed in 1965 as part of the Beeching cuts (see box, page 96). The station was not near any major population centres; rather, it was built because the railway traversed nearby Baynards Park, a country estate owned by Lord Thurlow, who insisted on a station being built here in return for allowing the line across his land. The station was used as a location for the 1957 BBC Television adaptation of *The Railway Children* and movies such as *The Grass is Greener*, where Cary Grant is seen walking along the platforms. The station is now in private ownership, and they have done a wonderful job of restoring it. You cannot access it, but you can see some of it by looking over the waist-height fence. The owners ask that you do not take photos of any of the buildings as this is their home. Once you turn left at the railway station, you are now on NCN223. Follow this for the next 11km along the route once taken by trains along the **Cranleigh line**.

When a railway is built, layers of compacted material are laid down in advance for ballast, before sleepers and rails are placed in position. The rails and sleepers are only held in place by their own weight so that, when they are removed, all that is left is the ground beneath. You will find that when you ride down this section of the Cranleigh line, you are riding on earth and not a tarmac track. This means the old railway line can be a bit muddy in places. It is easy to see why the line was closed: the route passes through countryside most of the time you will be riding along it (see box, page 96). Do note the occasional piece of railway infrastructure, like a bridge, still crossing what was once the railway. After 4km, you will pass a metal gate as you are now entering **Cranleigh** village. On your right is Snoxhall Play Park, and you will come to the first piece of tarmac since

↑ The historic well in Cranleigh market square (Charles Bowman/S)

Baynards Station. This road is called Snoxhall Fields. You are not on this for long because, as the road bears to the left, you need to continue straight on, following NCN223. You will come to John Wiskar Drive. Turn left on to this and then another left on to Knowle Lane. You will be taking an almost immediate right and then right again to get back on to NCN223.

Unlike Baynards, Cranleigh Station was demolished. The remains of the platforms can still be seen (if you look hard enough) behind the shops that took its place. If you have the time, there are some interesting sites to see on the High Street. At the eastern end is the **obelisk**, which is now a mile post, but was built to celebrate the building of a new road in an area where the countryside was almost unpassable in the winter. Near to where the station once stood is **Fountain Square** and its water fountain, on top of which stands a carving of a crane. The village gets its name from the bird, which is part of the parish council's coat of arms. It is also worth visiting ❼ **St Nicolas Church**. Not only is it a lovely building, but carved into one of the pillars is an unusual feature: the face of a smiling cat. We can't credit it for influencing Lewis Carroll, who spent considerable time in nearby Guildford visiting his sisters, because he had already published *Alice in Wonderland* before he set foot in the area.

Continue along the trail where you will also pass over and ride parallel to the remains of the Wey & Arun Canal (see Ride 7, page 87). After 6.3km, look right where there is a wooden fence going down a slope. Turn right but be careful when descending as the trail bears to the left and you need to take a sharp right when you reach the bottom. You are now on NCN22. Follow this as you pass between some fields until you reach a post with a sign for the NCN22 and an arrow pointing right. Follow the trail right and on to Lordshill Road. Shortly after this, turn left on to Hullbrook Lane for just over 800m. You will soon arrive at **Shamley Green**, once the home of film director Alfred Hitchcock. At the junction, turn left on to Guildford Road (B2128) which is also part of the Surrey Cycleway. In another 800m, turn right on to Northcote Lane.

This is mostly a single-track road but there are passing points to let traffic go by. You will also be cycling uphill, but it is nowhere near as long as the one you completed earlier in the ride. After 900m, you will come to a T-junction. Turn left on to Littleford Lane where you will continue to cycle uphill and be cycling through **Blackheath Common** once again. Once you start to cycle downhill, you will once more come to Blackheath village. Continue straight along this road until you reach the crossroads when you will be on Sampleoak Lane. In just over 1km, you will be back at Chilworth Station and the end of the ride.

THE ESSENTIALS

GETTING THERE By train, Chilworth is a 53-minute journey from London Waterloo, with a change at Guildford. By car, Chilworth is 6km southeast of Guildford along the A281 and A248.

FACILITIES There are public toilets in Cranleigh village, located on Village Way near Snoxhall Play Park.

WHERE TO EAT

The Bulls Head Inn, The Street, Ewhurst, GU6 7QD; ✆ 01483 277447; ⟁ thebullsheadinn. co.uk. This Edwardian inn serves a wide selection of meals, with snacks and lighter options also available. See the menus on the website for details. It serves lunch and dinner all week except Sun, when the kitchen is open in the afternoon only. £–££

Aliment Juicery, Stocklund Sq, 174 High St, Cranleigh, GU6 8RG; ✆ 07796 932643; ⟁ alimentjuicery.co.uk; closed Mon. Specialising in healthy cold-press juices (see the website for details), they have a lovely selection of homemade cakes along with light bites. Vegetarian and vegan options are also available. I can recommend the BLT wrap and Black Lemonade. £–££

Forge On The Green, The Old Forge, Shamley Green, GU5 0UB; ⟁ forgeonthegreen.co.uk; closed Thu. Based in a beautiful building, this social enterprise café provides opportunities for young people with additional needs to gain workplace experience and skills. Light bites with seasonal dishes and weekly specials. The bacon baps and cinnamon buns are very popular. £

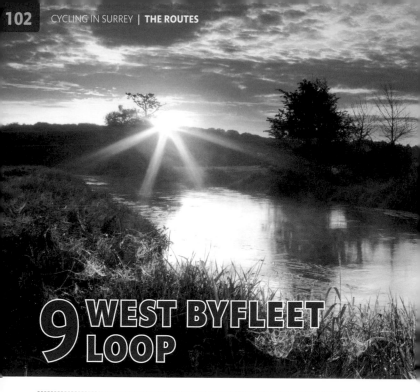

9 WEST BYFLEET LOOP

START/FINISH	West Byfleet Railway Station
DISTANCE/TIME	17.8km/2hrs (extension: 5.6km, 30mins)
DIFFICULTY/TERRAIN	② A flat ride along B-roads, with 25% off-road; some short sections on A-roads
SCENIC RATING	© River towpath, historic churches, an Elizabethan summer house and RHS Garden Wisley (on extension)
SUITABLE FOR	MTB, gravel or sturdy hybrid (with off-road tyres)
CYCLE ROUTE	A3 Cycle Route, Venus Trail, Surrey Cycleway
MAPS	OS Explorer 145 and 160 (1:25 000)
KOMOOT REF	879211816

↑ Sunrise over Newark Priory (BrianOrman/S)

This ride takes you along several Surrey cycle routes. You will see beautiful Norman churches and the historic village of Ripley. It also takes in a section of the River Wey, near where you will catch sight of a ruined abbey. While following the river, you will cross land without a towpath, which is marshy and difficult to ride on, so use footwear which you don't mind being covered in mud.

THE ROUTE

Come out on the southern side of ❶ **West Byfleet Station** and turn left. Follow the road around and then turn right on Madeira Road. Take a left on to Station Approach and, at the traffic lights, go straight over Old Woking Road (A245) and on to Pyrford Road for 1.3km. This is part of the Venus Trail cycling route. Turn right on to Boltons Lane and then right again on to Engliff Lane. At the end of Engliff Lane, you will see on

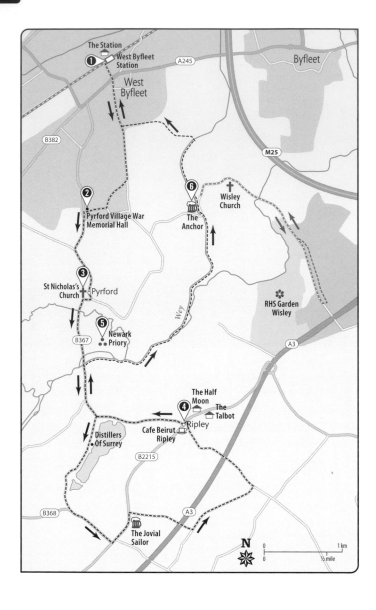

your right a sign for **Pyrford Village** and its ❷ **War Memorial Hall**. The sign includes a painting of a pear tree, as 'Pyrford' is derived from Old English and means 'the ford by the pear tree'.

Turn left on to Upshot Lane (B367), on which you will be following a section of the cycle route used during the 2012 Olympic road races. At the T-junction look across the road to your right and you will see a small **standing stone**. This was once a boundary stone, and local legend says that it moves around at midnight. Turn left on to Church Hill (B367). For the next 2.2km, you will be following the Surrey Cycleway. As the road slopes downwards, ahead of you is the historic ❸ **St Nicholas's Church**, a Grade I listed building and a beautiful example of a Norman church, having been built in the mid-1100s. The medieval ochre frescoes inside were covered in whitewash for hundreds of years.

Turn right out of the church and continue heading along Church Hill. As the road bears to the left, you will now be in Newark Lane. As you pass over the **Bourne Stream Bridge** (which actually crosses over Hoe Stream, confusingly), on your left poking through the vegetation is the ruin of **Newark Priory** (see below). Ride across the single-track bridge

↑ Church of St Nicholas, Pyrford (Ross Hamilton)

RIPLEY: 'THE MECCA FOR ALL GOOD CYCLISTS'

So said Lord Bury in 1887. In the latter years of the 19th century, the latest trend for the leisured classes was bicycle riding, and one route that gained worldwide attention was the **Ripley Ride**, starting at The Angel pub in Thames Ditton and finishing ten miles later at The Anchor in Ripley. So popular was this ride that it attracted 20,000 cyclists in 1894, according to local police estimates. But its once-quiet country lanes are now major A-roads.

A few doors down from The Anchor is **St Mary Magdalen**, which became known as the 'Parish Church of Cycling'. As you go in, in front of you is the Cyclists' Window, below which is a brass plaque dedicated to the Dibble family; Mrs Dibble and her daughters ran The Anchor during the heyday of the Ripley Ride. A further memorial to cycling in the church commemorates Herbert Liddell Cortis, believed to be the first person to ride 20 miles in under an hour.

↑ Cyclists outside The Anchor in Ripley, 1896 (Send & Ripley History Society)

over the River Wey and continue along Newark Lane. You'll soon pass
The Seven Stars pub, one of many in this area with a nautical name. The
main road between London and the Royal Navy base at Portsmouth once
passed through Ripley, and a nautical name may have been thought useful
in attracting business from passing sailors.

Turn right on to Polesden Lane. The road is surrounded by trees and
hedges but is quite narrow, so be mindful of vehicles. After 200m, on your
left you will see a gate and a sign for **Distillers Of Surrey**. This is located
next to **Papercourt Lake**, which is a lovely place to stop and watch the
local wildlife. If you have room in your bag, make sure you take away a
bottle of their lovely gin.

Bear to the left in order to stay on Polesden Lane. You will soon reach
the hamlet of **Send Marsh** with its nice mix of modern and older houses,
with some of the oldest located around the village green, which will be
on your right. Send Marsh has no church or shops, but it does have one
pub, called The Saddlers Arms.

At the tip of the village green, you will reach a T-junction. Turn left,
following the sign to Ripley. You are now on Send Marsh Road (B368).
At the end of the road, turn left on to the Portsmouth Road (B2215). This
is quite a busy B-road, but there is a clearly marked bike lane because it
is on the A3 Cycle Route. Turn right after The Jovial Sailor pub and on to
Grove Heath Road. You pass over the A3 and the road bears to the left.
The road is quiet, but watch out for pot-holes. At the end of the road, turn
left on to Rose Lane. Passing over the A3 once more, the road bears to the
left and you will be entering the village of ❹ **Ripley**. On the right at the
end of Rose Lane is The Bakery, whose double-sausage, double-bacon,
double-egg baguette is well worth stopping for.

One thing you are guaranteed to see in and around Ripley are other
cyclists. Down the High Street to your left is **The Anchor** pub, which was
the final stop for 19th-century cyclists completing the Ripley Ride (see
box opposite). The Anchor of the late Victorian era had a reputation for
accommodating any cyclists who arrived at the door, no matter what the
hour. Apart from much-needed liquid refreshment, the out-of-hours
menu for weary travellers consisted of cold meats. One traveller arriving

very late at night asked if any of these meats could be warmed up but was informed that only the mustard was hot. Out-of-hours hospitality only went so far.

Turn left on to the High Street (B2215), and then an almost immediate right on to Newark Lane. As you travel along the road, you will see a beautiful gatehouse on your right. This is the entrance to **Dunsborough Park**, a country estate with 25ha of landscaped gardens (see ⌖ dunsboroughpark.com for opening hours). Soon, you will find yourself back at the bridge over the **River Wey** you crossed earlier. Once over the bridge, turn right and follow the towpath. It is from here that you will have the clearest view of the ruins of ❺ **Newark Priory**, as well as the closest, it being on private land. The priory was established in the late 1100s and dissolved during the reign of Henry VIII.

Crossing back over the river, you will come to a gate. Pass through, but be warned that there's no towpath for the next 500m so you may be forced to walk some of it if the ground is particularly muddy. Once you pass through the next gate, the towpath resumes. When you get to the weir, cross over it and turn right, going past the lock-keeper's cottage. This

↑ Dunsborough Park gatehouse (Ross Hamilton)

is the **Walsham Gates**, with a sign on the side of the house to tell you it was opened in 1653 and is the last remaining turf-sided lock on the Wey.

Stay on this side of the river and continue along the path. Look out for a curious building on the other bank. This is the **Summer House of John Donne**, the famous poet and polymath who lived on this estate during the latter days of Elizabeth I. You will soon reach **Pyrford Lock** and another pub called ❻ **The Anchor**. From here, you can elect to take the extension, a small detour to Wisley (see below).

Continue along the Wey Navigation for 1km and cross the river at the first bridge you come to after The Anchor. It's steep and you might need to walk your bike over. You are now back on the Venus Trail. Cycle through the trees and then over the field until you reach Dodd's Lane. Turn right and head along Pyrford Road once again, this time in the other direction. Cross straight over at the traffic lights, back on to Station Approach, and you will soon be at West Byfleet Station again and the end of the ride.

EXTENSION: RHS GARDEN WISLEY

At The Anchor, near Pyrford Lock, follow the road to the right. This is Wisley Lane, which is also part of the Venus Trail. It's a narrow road, so stay as far to the left as you can. At Wisley, pull into the small car park at the brown sign for **Wisley Church**. Like St Nicholas's, earlier on the ride, this is a beautiful 12th-century church. There is a booklet detailing its history just inside the door.

Turn right to rejoin Wisley Lane. You will soon see that the hedge on the right-hand side of the road gives way to a metal fence. This is the boundary to **RHS Garden Wisley**. A ride of a further 1km takes you to the entrance. For anyone interested in horticulture, and who wishes to view the work of the country's foremost gardening charity, this detour is a must. Here you can see one of the largest plant collections in the world. The Glasshouse (a multi-temperature experience), Bowles' Corner (a collection of unusual plants chosen by former RHS President E A Bowles) and the Walled Gardens are among its many highlights. (The café is recommended, too.) To return to the main ride, go back the way you came.

THE ESSENTIALS

GETTING THERE By train, the journey from London Waterloo is 28 minutes on a fast train or 43 minutes on a slow one. By car, West Byfleet is 6km from the A3 (Painshill Junction) and then along the A245.

FACILITIES Public toilets are available on Lavender Park Road near West Byfleet Station.

WHERE TO EAT

Cafe Beirut Ripley, 1–2 London Hse, High St, Ripley, GU23 6AA; ✆ 01483 224252; closed Mon. This lovely family-run café is a great place to refuel. Light bites as well as a selection of cold

↑ RHS Wisley (BBA Photography/S)

and hot drinks are available. Everything on the menu is available to take away. **£**

The Anchor, High St, Ripley, Woking, GU23 6AE; 📞 01483 211866; 🖰 ripleyanchor.co.uk; closed Sun. Marking the destination of the Ripley Ride (page 106), the food is cooked by Michelin-trained chefs and is available to eat in only. Booking in advance is advised. **££**

The Anchor, Pyrford Lock, Wisley, GU23 6QW; 📞 01932 342507; 🖰 anchorpyrford. co.uk. Located next to Pyrford Lock on the Wey Navigation, there is plenty of outdoor seating for the cyclist in need of refreshment. The menu consists of full meals as well as light bites. **££**

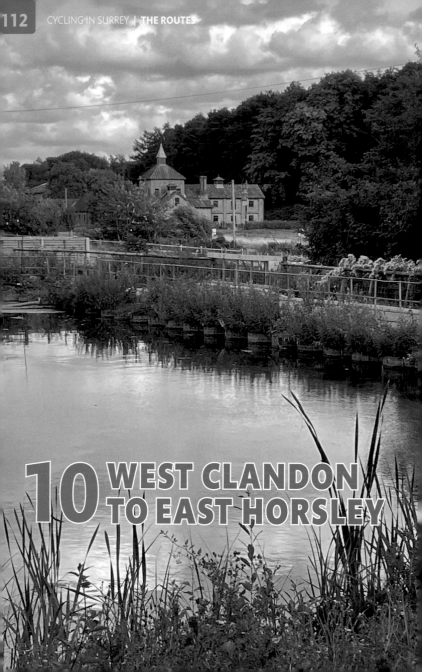

10 WEST CLANDON TO EAST HORSLEY

START	Clandon Railway Station
FINISH	Horsley Railway Station
DISTANCE/TIME	27.4km/2½hrs (extension: 3.47km, 30min round trip)
DIFFICULTY/TERRAIN	② An undulating ride following on- and off-road routes, crossing A-roads and riding along B-roads and country lanes
SCENIC RATING	© Passing through villages and peaceful countryside, encountering pubs and historic churches
SUITABLE FOR	MTB, gravel or sturdy hybrid (with off-road tyres)
CYCLE ROUTE	NCN22, Surrey Cycleway
MAPS	OS Explorer 145 and 146 (1:25 000)
KOMOOT REF	889056178

This is possibly the most challenging ride in the book and you will need a good level of fitness. There are long climbs, the off-road routes can be very muddy, and one downhill stretch is made up of loose stones. But the views are magnificent, and there are plenty of interesting sites and beautiful villages to see on this ride. It can be combined with Ride 11 (page 122), the 'figure-of-eight' near Ockham, as they share a section of road in West Horsley.

THE ROUTE

Come out of ❶ **Clandon Station** and head down Station Approach. Turn right on The Street (A247) and ride along it for 1.2km. As you reach the edge of the village of Clandon, you will see three white posts on your right. The sign on the other side of these posts shows the village name and an image of a dog attacking a dragon (see box, page 119). Turn right on to Green Lane. This road is not well maintained and, after 600m, it becomes a mud track which can be a bit tricky to navigate, especially after a lot of rain. At the junction, turn right on Ripley Road and you are now on the Surrey Cycleway. After 2.2km, you will be in the village of **East Clandon**, where the 1960s TV series *Catweazle* was filmed. Go past the war memorial and, at the junction, there is a left turn to **Hatchlands Park**, should you wish to visit it: a National Trust property which houses the Cobbe Collection of musical instruments and artworks (⊘ nationaltrust.org.uk). Apart from exploring the Georgian country house, there are 160ha of parklands and gardens, as well as a stone temple folly. The main entrance is along the Epsom Road (A246), which can be very busy, so take care if you choose that route.

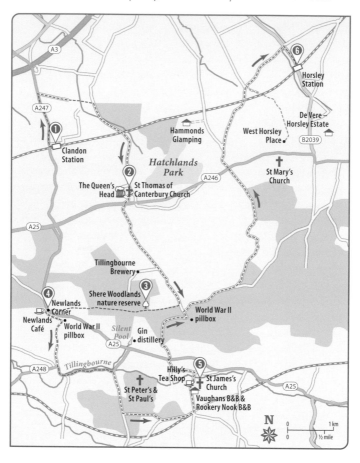

To follow our route, turn right and on to another road called The Street. To your right is the ❷ **St Thomas of Canterbury Church**. A stained-glass window depicting the last moments of the saint's life can be seen to your left as you walk through the door. The wonderful online history claims that a church has been on this site since the 7th century, but, like so many others in Surrey, it underwent major restoration in the Victorian era. Check out the artwork on the north aisle ceiling and the ornate tomb of Stuart, Baron Rendel of Hatchlands, below it.

Follow The Street until you come to the Epsom Road (A246). This can be very busy and there is no pedestrian crossing, so please be careful. Go straight across it and on to Staple Lane for the next 2.5km. This is a tough climb, but when you reach the top, make sure to look behind you for a spectacular view of northern Surrey. Coming down the other side, look out for a sign on your right for the **Tillingbourne Brewery**. If you are here on a Friday or Saturday when the brewery is open to visitors, pop in and purchase their Hop Troll IPA. You've earned it after that climb.

Turn right into the West Hanger Car Park. You are now entering the ❸ **Shere Woodlands nature reserve**. This is home to rare species such as the lemon slug and hazel dormouse, neither of which I saw on this ride – but I suppose the key word is 'rare'. This trail is part of the North Downs Way and, like the earlier trail, can be muddy. You will follow it for 2.6km passing by, but not seeing, the legendary **Silent Pool** and the distillery named after it (see box, page 119). There is a footpath down to the distillery, but it is dangerous and I would not recommend using it.

The Way emerges on Shere Road (A25). You need to cross this busy road to enter ❹ **Newlands Corner**. From here you will have a magnificent view of southern Surrey and you can find out about the area's wildlife in the visitor centre. The trail down from Newlands Corner is covered in loose stones, so be careful in your descent. As the trail takes a right, there is a World War II pillbox in front of you. After 1km on the trail, you will come to a tarmac road. This is Water Lane; when you reach the junction, turn left on to Chilworth Road (A248) and follow it for 1.3km. This will take you into the lovely village of **Albury**.

The road through the village is quite narrow for an A-road but do look out on the left for a large red-brick building. This is the old flour mill, once powered by the **River Tillingbourne**, which can be seen following the curve of the road. The river's source is near Leith Hill and it joins the River Wey near Guildford. Along its banks used to be several mills: the Tillingbourne Valley was a centre of industry for many centuries, which included the gunpowder mills in Chilworth (see Ride 7, page 89). In the early 20th century, the old Albury mill was repurposed so it could generate electricity for the village before being converted into apartments.

Out of the village, take a right on to New Road where you will see a brown sign for a historic church on the Albury Estate. Turn left here on to Albury Park and make your way to the church of **St Peter and St Paul**. A church has occupied this site since Saxon times, but the oldest part of the current building dates to the 13th century. It was pretty much left to fall apart from 1840, but it is now maintained by The Churches Conservation Trust which has looked after it since 1974, replacing the roof and restoring it to such a degree that services are held on holy days such as Christmas and Easter. The church has many interesting features, including

↑ The view from Newlands Corner (Alex Manders/S)

a 15th-century wall painting of St Christopher, a brass commemorating the knight John Weston, and the stained glass in the Drummond Chapel. The exterior of this building was used in the film *Four Weddings and a Funeral*. **Albury Park** itself contains a Victorian manor house (now converted into apartments) as well as a landscape garden designed by John Evelyn in the 17th century. Unfortunately, the house and gardens are private property and cannot be visited by the public. Confusingly, Albury has two churches, both called St Peter's and St Paul's. The modern church dates to 1840 and can be found in the modern village, up Church Lane which is opposite Pratt's Stores. Though an impressive building to look at, it tends to be open only when in use.

When you leave the church, ride back the way you came and turn left to rejoin New Road, which you will be on for 1km. This is another climb; once you are over the summit, you will need to take a left on to Park Road. You will be on the Surrey Cycleway again, and the NCN22. Park Road becomes Little London; when you come to the junction, turn left on to

↑ The original Church of St Peter and St Paul in Albury (Ross Hamilton)

Sandy Lane. You will soon enter the village of **Shere** – a picturesque village, with many lovely buildings (including The White Horse pub, the church and several cottages). It has featured in numerous TV shows and films – the earliest dating from 1899! Take a right to visit ❺ **St James's Church** and see the plaque commemorating Christine Carpenter, the Anchoress of Shere. Anchoresses were women who chose a life of religious seclusion and deprivation. A stone cell was built for Christine on the north side of the church, her intention to spend the rest of her days inside it. Inside the church, two slots are visible in the wall of her cell: one, the 'quatrefoil', through which she would have received the Blessed Sacrament; the other an angled 'squint', through which she could see the altar. She entered the cell in 1329 but she had a change of mind and managed to leave as the cell had a door. She did return, though, for fear of excommunication. Some sources say she went back willingly; others say she was forced against her will.

On leaving the church, head back through The Square and turn right on to Middle Street. Just before you need to turn left on to Upper Street, look in the wall on your left. There you will see the **Shere Well and Water Fountain**, which was running dry when I passed it. Follow Upper Street until you reach Shere Road (A25). You need to turn right and then an almost immediate left on to Combe Lane. The A25 is very busy and there isn't any provision made for cyclists here. This is the toughest climb of the ride, but when the road flattens out you will see another World War II pillbox in front of you. Follow the road around to the left and then take a right to stay on Combe Lane. In 1.2km, turn left on to another Shere Road. Unlike the previous one, this is a quiet country back road, and for the next 2.5km you will see little in the way of houses but you will have a pleasant ride through some lovely countryside. Apart from one small climb, the route is now downhill.

At the roundabout, cross the Epsom Road (A246) again and into **West Horsley** along a road called The Street. When you see the road sign on your left for Ripley Lane, for the next 2.6km you will be following a stretch of road which you will also cover in Ride 11 (page 122), but in the opposite direction. The road changes its name to East Lane; when

LOCAL LEGENDS

Every county in England has its fair share of legends, and Surrey is no different. There are two attached to the area we have travelled on this ride. The first concerns West Clandon and is commemorated in the village sign: the one on which a dog and a dragon are locked in combat. The story behind the sign dates to the 1700s when a soldier who had deserted from the army came, with his dog, to the village. Here he heard the tale of a dragon causing distress to the local residents. He offered to rid West Clandon of the dragon and asked in return that he might be spared punishment for his desertion. The village agreed. After a long fight, which he would have lost but for the intervention of his dog, the soldier killed the beast with his bayonet.

The second legend concerns the Silent Pool, from which the local gin distillery, located beside the pool, takes its name. It is said that no bird sings near the pool because it is haunted by the ghost of a young lady who drowned in its waters. The story takes place during the reign of King John. The King himself is said to have ridden past the lake and spied the young lady swimming. Seeing the King, and fearing that he wished to have his wicked way with her, she made her way to the pool's deeper parts. Unable to swim, she sank, and the King did nothing to save her. Her ghost has been reported to appear at night.

you reach the end of it, turn right on to Ockham Road North (B2039). After you pass under a railway bridge, there is a sign for ❻ **Horsley Station** Turn left on to Station Approach and you have reached the end of the ride.

EXTENSION: WEST HORSLEY PLACE

A building has occupied this site since Anglo-Saxon times, although the current house dates to the 16th century. The house was in private ownership until 2014, when it was inherited by legendary quizmaster Bamber Gascoigne who had it restored and turned into a charitable trust. To get there, turn right down Lollesworth Lane and cross the railway bridge. Turn left at the end of the bridge and then right. Follow the bridle lane and you will be entering the rear entrance to the West Horsley Place Estate. Apart from the Grade I-listed manor house, with its great beauty and historical significance, the estate is also home to a diverse range of flora and fauna, a complete list of which can be found on the website (⊘ westhorsleyplace.org). There is also a 700-seat 'Theatre in the Woods', hosting live theatre, ballet and concerts (⊘ grangeparkopera.co.uk).

If you wish to continue exploring, travel out of the main entrance to West Horsley Place (to the A246) and look right. **St Mary's Church** is said to be haunted by a ghostly head, believed to be that of Sir Walter Raleigh. This is indeed where the head of the Elizabethan explorer is buried: West Horsley Place was where Sir Walter's wife and son lived after his decapitation.

To return to the route, retrace your steps back to Lollesworth Lane and turn right on to The Street.

THE ESSENTIALS

GETTING THERE By train, the journey from London Waterloo to Clandon is approximately 55 minutes depending on which one you catch. By car, the station is 8km from Guildford town centre, via the A25 and then the A247.

FACILITIES Both Clandon and Horsley stations have public toilets, but these are only open when the ticket office is. There are public toilets at the car park at Newlands Corner and the Old Fire Station building on Middle Street, Shere.

WHERE TO EAT

The Queen's Head, The Street, East Clandon, GU4 7RY; ☎ 01483 222332; ⊘ queensheadeastclandon.co.uk. Dating to the 1500s, this old coaching inn still has its stable building in what is now the car park. The kitchen is open all day for full meals but light bites such as sandwiches are only available at lunchtime. **£–££**

Newland's Café, Newland's Corner, Albury, GU4 8SE. Serves light bites and has a wonderful selection of cakes. Well worth stopping off – not only for the food but the rather stunning view. **£**
Hilly's Tea Shop, The Square, Shere, GU5 9HG; ☎ 01483 346550; ⊘ hillysteashop.com; closed Mon. Serving a selection of homemade cakes and light bites, they also sell local honey. **£**

The award-winning Slow Travel series from Bradt Guides

Over 30 regional guides across Britain.
See the full list at bradtguides.com/slowtravel.

11 EFFINGHAM JUNCTION LOOP

START/FINISH	Effingham Junction Railway Station
DISTANCE/TIME	19.9km/2hrs (extension: 5.3km round trip, 30mins)
DIFFICULTY/TERRAIN	② Level or rolling terrain on B-roads and country lanes; 12% is off-road on Ockham Common
SCENIC RATING	Ⓐ Country roads, the last semaphore tower in England, a historic church, woodland, and a common
SUITABLE FOR	MTB, gravel or sturdy hybrid (with off-road tyres)
CYCLE ROUTE	None on this ride
MAPS	OS 145 Explorer (1:25 000)
KOMOOT REF	873153331

tarting off near to the suburban village of Effingham Junction, you will ride past the Norman church of All Saints in Ockham and the last remaining semaphore tower in Britain. You will also pass several pubs, one of which has appeared in a few famous films. This ride includes hedgerow-lined country roads, where you will be surrounded by farmland and the occasional hamlet. The extension takes you to a stunning example of 18th-century garden design.

THE ROUTE

Turn left out of ❶ **Effingham Junction Station** and make your way on to Howard Road. You will pass over the railway bridge and soon come to a T-junction. Turn left on to Forest Road and you will be riding through the village of **Effingham Junction**. Continue for 500m, taking a right turning into The Drift. You are now riding through a nature reserve. It is managed by the Surrey Wildlife Trust and known as **The Forest and The Highlands**. Over 150 plant species have been recorded here, along with 50 species of birds (including woodpeckers and tawny owls) and land animals such as field voles and roe deer.

The Drift is 1.3km long; when you reach its end, you will see a sign on the left for 'East Horsley Village: The Lovelace Village' (see Ride 13,

← The Semaphore Tower on Ockham Common (cooperman/S)

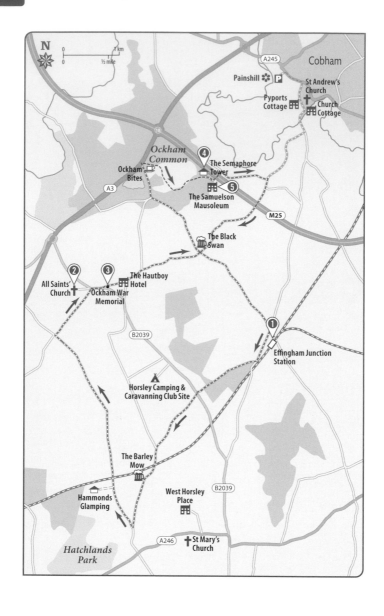

N

0   1 km
0   ½ mile

A245

Cobham

Painshill

P

St Andrew's
Church

Pyports
Cottage

Church
Cottage

*Ockham
Common*

④ The Semaphore
Tower

Ockham
Bites

⑤

A3

The Samuelson
Mausoleum

M25

The Black
Swan

② All Saints'
Church

③

The Hautboy
Hotel

Ockham War
Memorial

① Effingham Junction
Station

B2039

Horsley Camping &
Caravanning Club Site

The Barley
Mow

Hammonds
Glamping

West Horsley
Place

B2039

*Hatchlands
Park*

A246

St Mary's
Church

page 140). This section is also part of Ride 10 (page 112). Take a left and then turn immediately right into East Lane. You are now in the village of **West Horsley**. From now on, the buildings become sparser, and in 800m you will see a left turn on to Lollesworth Lane, which will take you to **West Horsley Place** (see Ride 10, page 119). Continuing straight on instead, the road name changes to The Street. 750m after passing under the railway bridge, turn right on to Ripley Lane. There are very few buildings on this lane; on your left, you will see an ornate gate which, if opened, would lead you through to **Hatchlands Park** (see Ride 10, page 114). Continue along Ripley Lane for 3.6km and then turn right on to Guileshill Lane where a signpost will direct you towards Ockham. This section of road was used during the road races at the 2012 Olympics.

Continue along this road until you reach a T-junction. You will see a road sign opposite you with 'Ockham Road North' written on it. However, before turning right, look behind you and you will see a sign for ❷ **All Saints Church**. This church dates to 1160; William of Ockham (see box, page 126) is believed to have lived on the site. There is a window dedicated to him and above the altar is a rare feature: the east window has seven lancets. The only other church in the country to share this feature is St Nicholas, Blakeney in Norfolk. There is also a memorial plaque dedicated to Stephen Lushington, MP. A noted judge, he was also a keen advocate for the abolition of the slave trade.

Having now turned right, you will be on Ockham Road North (B2039); after 300m, you will see the ❸ **Ockham war memorial**. Turn left at the memorial into Ockham Lane. After a further 400m, you will come across a stunning red-brick building: the former pub **The Hautboy Hotel** (a hautboy is a musical instrument and precursor of the oboe). Not so long ago, this pub was a stop-off for cyclists on the Ripley Ride (see Ride 9, page 106) who were looking for a room for the night, particularly those unable to find one in Ripley itself. In 1898, the pub made the news when the landlord refused entry to Lady Harberton who was out for a bike ride. Her crime was to have been wearing 'exceedingly baggy knickerbockers reaching below the knee'. The pub has now been converted into luxury flats.

WILLIAM OF OCKHAM

William of Ockham is remembered today for the 'razor' that has been attributed to him. 'Ockham's Razor' is a problem-solving principle whereby the simplest explanation is the preferred option. We cannot be sure of the exact location and date of his birth, but we know William received training in philosophy and logic at Greyfriars (London) before becoming a subdeacon in Southwark (then part of Surrey but now very much in London). In 1307, he began his studies at Oxford University. William then became embroiled in a dispute that led to the dismissal of John Lutterell, the then Chancellor of the University. Lutterell did not take his dismissal lightly and took his grievances to the Pope, accusing William of heresy. The latter was summoned by the Pope to appear before a commission in Avignon to answer to the charges.

William put up a stout defence but was kept in Avignon, essentially under house arrest. He eventually escaped from Avignon and ended up at the court of Louis IV of Bavaria, the Holy Roman Emperor. William died in 1347 and was buried in the Franciscan cemetery in Munich. Although William of Ockham is forever associated with the above-mentioned razor, it does not appear in any of his writings but rather seems to have been introduced in the 17th century by John Punch, an Irish Franciscan theologian.

Continue along Ockham Lane until you reach a crossroads. Opposite you is **The Black Swan** pub. The pub makes an appearance in the film *Performance*, which starred Mick Jagger; rumour has it that the interiors were also used in the film *An American Werewolf in London*, where it was known as 'The Slaughtered Lamb'. Turn left on to Old Lane and cycle for 1.5km until you see the entrance to a car park on your right. Ride past this until you see the entrance to another – Ockham Common Bolder Mere Car Park – also on your right. Turn into it in order to access Ockham Common.

Ockham Common is also managed by the Surrey Wildlife Trust and is home to birds such as the hobby, goldcrest and nightjar. Other creatures to keep an eye out for are dragonflies, the common lizard and snakes, including adders. Cycling is permitted but it is important to follow the designated route so as not to disturb the wildlife, especially the nightjar, which makes its nest on the ground. The route out of the car park takes you gently uphill; this is where some grip on your tyres will help because the terrain is sandy. It is important to follow the route as shown on komoot as it easy to miss the ❹ **Semaphore Tower** on top of Telegraph Hill (/// spike. pill.seated). Its purpose was to transmit information by semaphore from London to the naval dockyards at Portsmouth: messages would take about 15 minutes to get from one place to the other. Today, the building can be booked for self-catering holidays via the Landmark Trust (see *Accommodation*, page 227).

There is a paved road in front of the tower, which you're going to ride down. As the road bears round to the left, you will see a solitary wooden pillar on your right. This is the start of a dirt track. If you fancy doing a little bit of exploring in the woods, you can look for the ❺ **Samuelson Mausoleum** (/// drag.chase.crown). It was commissioned by Sir Henry Samuelson in 1919 to house the remains of his family, though no bodies remain there today. I found this path easier to walk than cycle.

Having picked up the road again, you'll find it going downhill all the way to a bridge over the M25. At the end of this road, which has no name, is a locked gate which you can go around. Turn right on to Pointers Road; after 800m, you will reach a T-junction. A left turn will take you on the extension to Painshill (see below). A right turn will take you back down Ockham Lane, where, after 1.8km, you will be back at The Black Swan pub. Turn left on to Old Lane.

Following this road for 1.7km takes you back to the village of Effingham Junction. At the end of Old Lane, turn right on to Horsley Road and then immediately left on to Howard Road. Effingham Junction Railway Station will be on your right.

EXTENSION: PAINSHILL PARK

This extension takes you to a beautiful example of the English Landscape Movement, as well giving you a glimpse of historic Cobham. Turn left at the end of Pointers Road and make your way along Plough Lane for

1.2km. Once you pass The Plough Inn (which will be on your right), you will reach a T-junction. Turn left on to Downside Road. The road bears to the right, passing over the River Mole. In front of you, you will see a white house, home between 1814 and 1851 to William Watt, a renowned artist and engraver; a blue plaque attests to this. The road bears to the left at Watt's old house and on your right is **St Andrew's Church** which dates from the 1100s although it is believed that the bell-tower could be even older, maybe dating to the 800s; in which case it would be a rare example of an Anglo-Saxon building.

Opposite the entrance to the church is **Pyports Cottage**, a Grade II-listed building. On the wall next to the pedestrian entrance is a blue plaque listing several previous occupants. The most recent on the list is Vernon Lushington, who lived at Pyports between 1877 and 1903, and was a lawyer, Second Secretary to the Admiralty, and friendly with members of the Pre-Raphaelite movement. His daughter Kitty was a friend of Virginia Woolf and the inspiration for the character of Mrs Dalloway in Woolf's novel of the same name. Back on the route, you'll find the road bears round to the right.

Downside Bridge Road can be busy. But, once you pass the last house on the left, there is sign for a public footpath. Follow the path as it runs through the wonderfully named Leg O'Mutton Field and continue until

↑ The Serpentine Lake in Painshill Park (John Gilham/S)

you reach Loriners Close. Turn right; at the end of Loriners Close is a T-junction. Turn left on to Between Streets (A245) and the entrance to **Painshill** is a few metres on the left.

Painshill was created by Charles Hamilton (no relation to me!) during the formative years of the English Landscape Movement, in which gardens were created that showcased an idealised view of nature. The garden has numerous features and follies including a Gothic tower, a Chinese bridge and a hermitage. At the time it was built, it was fashionable to have an actual hermit live in gardens such as this. The hermit employed by Hamilton was given a seven-year contract, but he only lasted a few weeks, having been spotted drinking in a local pub. Tickets must be bought in advance of a visit via the website (⊘ painshill.co.uk).

To return to the main ride, go back the way you came.

THE ESSENTIALS

GETTING THERE By train, Effingham Junction is roughly a 45-minute journey from London Waterloo. By car, it is 4.5km from Junction 10 of the M25, going via the A3 and Old Lane.

FACILITIES There are public toilets at Ockham Common in the same building as Ockham Bites; they are only open when the café is open. There are also toilets in the pubs that you pass.

WHERE TO EAT

Ockham Bites, Old Lane, Cobham, KT11 1NA; ⊘ 01932 866641. Open seven days a week. According to the *Surrey Advertiser* newspaper, this serves the best bacon butty around, even though the owner says it is more of a sandwich. It does serve more than bacon butties, though. **£**
The Barley Mow, 181 The Street, West Horsley, KT24 6HR; ⊘ 01483 282693; ⊘ barleymowhorsley.com. A classic English country pub with a large garden to the side.

Light bites and an English menu (only) at lunchtime, and Thai food (only) in the evening. The 'About Us' section of the website has an interesting history of the pub. **£–££**
The Black Swan, Old Lane, Ockham, KT11 1NG; ⊘ 01932 862364; ⊘ blackswanockham.com. This lovely country pub has a beautiful garden to enjoy their rather fine food. It is recommended that you book in advance as it can be busy all year round. **££**

12 GOMSHALL LOOP

START/FINISH	Gomshall Railway Station
DISTANCE/TIME	20.8km/2hrs (extension: 5.6km round trip, 30mins)
DIFFICULTY/TERRAIN	② An undulating ride with one climb up to the summit of Holmbury Hill; you will ride along B-roads, country lanes and some off-road paths
SCENIC RATING	⑧ The Hurtwood and the magnificent view from its summit; villages, historic churches and an Iron Age fort
SUITABLE FOR	MTB, electric bike, gravel or sturdy hybrid (with off-road tyres)
CYCLE ROUTE	NCN22, Surrey Cycleway
MAPS	OS Explorer 145 and 146 (1:25 000)
KOMOOT REF	888477326

↑ The Gomshall Mill pub (William Barton/S)

One of the shorter rides in this book, what it lacks in distance it makes up for in beauty. You will pass through several villages as you ride down the country lanes. You can also visit the remains of an Iron Age fort, some historic churches, and another of Surrey's lost castles. The extension takes you to Surrey's largest waterfall.

THE ROUTE

Leaving ❶ **Gomshall Station** head down Station Approach until you reach Station Road (A25). Turn right and make your way along the road, noting Coach House Surrey antique shop soon on your left, in front of which is an interesting display of carved wooden animals (such as horses, deer and the odd dinosaur). Next door is Vintage Frog antiques shop, also home to Albert's Coffee Bar (see below). Continue along Station Road until you reach **The Gomshall Mill** pub on your left. Turn left on to Goose Green and you are crossing the **River Tillingbourne**. The river runs directly under the pub: this 17th-century building was a working mill until 1953 and the waterwheel is still inside. Since the Middle Ages, the Tillingbourne Valley supported numerous industries including tanning, blacksmithing, corn production and gunpowder (see Ride 7, page 82).

Continue along Goose Green but be careful as this road is quite narrow and buses can come from the opposite direction. The road bends to the right and you are now on High View and briefly on NCN22. Just before the road bends to the left, you will see a wooden bus shelter, which also doubles up as the local book swap. Follow the road, now Queen Street, as it veers to the left. Once you cross the railway lines, it becomes Burrows Lane. Follow this narrow country lane for 850m until you reach the junction. Turn left on to Burrows Cross and then right on to Lawbrook Lane. Follow this single-track road for 2.2km until you come to another road junction. Take the left turn on to Walking Bottom. There are quite a few places in England that have the word 'bottom' in their name, but there are no connotations of anything rude. It derives from the Old English word *botm*, which means the ground, foundation or abyss. After a lovely ride down a gentle slope, you will soon come to the beautiful village of **Peaslake**.

The first building you will see on your right is ❷ **St Mark's Church**, which was built in the late 1800s. Looking at the outside of the building, there is an unusual steeple which houses a clock. Look left when you walk through the church door to see the mechanism that powers the clock. The church history says that the mechanism was manufactured in 1889 and has been running ever since with all its original parts. Some modernity has been added with an automatic winding system. Opposite the main door are saints' banners produced by the artist Margaret Tarrant. Tarrant lived in Peaslake for many years and is most famous for her book illustrations, which included *Alice in Wonderland* and *The Water Babies*, among others.

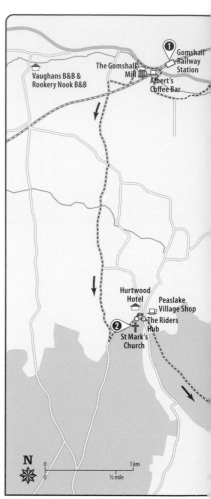

As the road bears around to the right, the large white building in front of you is the **Hurtwood Hotel** (see *Accommodation*, page 226). Opposite the inn is **The Riders Hub**, also known as Surrey Hills Bike Rental (see *Cycle Hire and Repairs*, page 229). Just past the Hurtwood Hotel is the village sign. Stay to the right of this and ahead is the **Peaslake Village Stores**. Not just a shop, it's the local Post Office, estate agent and art gallery, and it even does food and hot drinks to take away. Turn right at the war memorial on to Peaslake Lane and then take a left on to Radnor Road.

This single-track road climbs gently; after 1.3km, turn left on to the trail and you are in the

Hurtwood. You will be following an off-road track for the next 1.35km. Even though the Hurtwood is common land, it is still in private ownership. It has multiple unpaved cycling tracks of varying difficulty and, if you

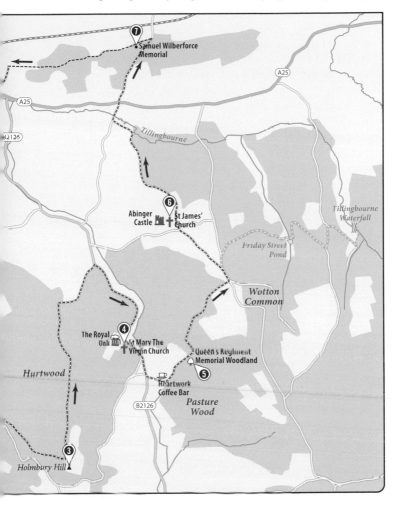

have the time, I recommend you explore them. ❸ **Holmbury Hill** is one of the highest points in Surrey and, on a clear day, you can see for up to 40km. The information board tells of all the sites you can see from this elevated position. You are also standing in the remains of an Iron Age fort.

Coming down, you first need to go back along part of the trail you travelled on the way up and then bear right. Follow it down for the next 2km. This is quite a wide trail and I found it the easiest to navigate. All the same, it is a bit sandy with rocks protruding out of the surface so be careful on your descent. At the base of the hill, the trail bears around to the right and you will come to a car park and then YHA Holbury St Mary on your left. Ride down the paved road which is called Radnor Lane. This slopes gently downhill, so watch your speed.

At the end of Radnor Lane, there is a sign pointing towards Holmbury St Mary. Turn right at this junction, joining Horsham Road (B2126). Having reached **Holmbury St Mary**, on your right on the other side of the green is **The Royal Oak** pub (see below). You will also see a church as the road bears to the left. ❹ **St Mary the Virgin Church** was designed by George Edmund Street, who was also responsible for the Royal Courts of Justice in London. The church was completed in 1879, and Street gifted the triptych, originally from Florence and dating to the late 1300s or early 1400s, which can be seen in the chancel. There is also a birthing tray, from the same era as the triptych. Birthing trays were elaborate presents given by members of the Florence elite to mark a new – but, more importantly, successful – birth.

Continuing along Horsham Road you will see a thatched roof structure on your left. It contains an old pump and was most probably the village well. If you look under the roof, you will see that someone has left a couple of fairy doors in the support posts. Turn left on to Pasture Wood Road; the second left turn will take you to the **Heartwork Coffee Bar** (see below). Follow the road as it bears to the left and slopes uphill. On your right is a sign to the ❺ **Queen's Regiment Memorial Woodland (QRMW)** (🖥 qrmw.org), which was designed to be a place of reflection and remembrance for members of all the UK's Armed Forces. Confusingly, it also calls itself the Quick Response Memorial Woodlands. Whatever the name, it is a registered charity designed to help ex-service personnel in need of assistance. Even though the site has an events programme, it can be visited outside of these times to be enjoyed as a tranquil space.

Leaving the QRMW, continue along Pasture Wood Road for just over 1km until you reach a T-junction. Turn left on to Leith Hill Road, which is part of the Surrey Cycleway, and ride along here until the next left turn which is Abinger Lane. Continue straight on, however, if you wish to explore the extension (see below).

As you make your way along Abinger Lane, you will see a small stone structure. This is **St James's Well**, built in 1893 by William John Evelyn, the lord of the manor. The well is no longer in use, but the mechanism is still *in situ* and can be seen behind the dedication. On your left, you will see a driveway with the word 'Goddards' embedded in the wall. Designed by Edwin Lutyens (see Ride 3, page 49), **Goddards** was designed as a holiday rest home for ladies without the means to afford one. The house is now part of the Landmark Trust property portfolio and can be visited on Wednesday afternoons from Easter to October (landmarktrust.org.uk).

Cycle on for 750m after Goddards and on your right you will see The Abinger Hatch, a 17th-century pub. On your left is ❻ **St James' Church**. As you make your way up the path to the church, look right and you will see the remains of the village stocks. According to the booklet that details the history of the church, these were used to punish boys who did not behave themselves during services. The church itself dates to the Middle Ages, with the Lady Chapel believed to have been built in the 1200s. Like many other churches in this book, this one had some major restoration work in the Victorian era. However, it also required additional work in the 20th century after a flying bomb exploded nearby in 1944, causing so much damage that the church did not reopen until 1951. And in 1966, the tower was struck by lightning, with the resulting fire burning through parts of the roof and the tower itself. You can also visit the remains of another of Surrey's castles here, but you will need to walk there. With the church entrance on your right, continue along the path until you reach a small metal gate. Go through the gate and follow the path as it bends to the right. On your left will be a mound of earth

SAMUEL WILBERFORCE

Samuel Wilberforce was the third son of William Wilberforce (see Ride 20, page 203), the noted campaigner for abolition of the slave trade. Samuel became a priest and managed to carve a successful career in his own right. His roles included Archdeacon of Surrey, which meant his primary residence was in Farnham Castle (see Ride 3, page 51), as well as Chaplain to Queen Victoria's husband, Prince Albert. A gifted speaker, he took part in the 1860 Oxford Evolution Debate where he challenged Darwin's theory of evolution. The monument on this ride marks the spot where Wilberforce died after falling from his horse.

covered in trees. This is the motte that was once **Abinger Castle** (/// soil. crazy.straw). Turn left out of the church and continue along Abinger Lane for 1.6km. At the T-junction, turn right on to Raikes Lane.

At the end of Raikes Lane, cross over the A25 on to White Down Lane. The A25 can be busy, so be careful when crossing it. After 900m, take a left at the sign for NCN22, entering the **Abinger Roughs**. The Roughs are an area of ancient woodland managed by the National Trust. If you wish to explore the woods further, you can follow the National Trust's tree trail, which includes local landmark the **Witch's Broom Tree** (⊘ nationaltrust. org.uk). Following the NCN22, you will soon come to an open area with a stone cross just left of the trail. This is the ❼ **Samuel Wilberforce**

↑ The Wilberforce Monument in Abinger Roughs (Ross Hamilton)

Memorial (see box opposite). 1.3km after the monument, you will reach a gate. Pass through this and continue along NCN 22. This is quite narrow and more like a footpath in comparison to your trails through the Roughs thus far. Hopefully, you will not get stuck behind a small herd of cows, which is what happened to me the first time I rode down here. You will come to a sign for NCN22, telling you to turn left. You will now be on Hackhurst Lane.

The road slopes gently downhill but watch your speed as this is a single-track road and cars can come in the opposite direction. You will soon be in the village of **Abinger Hammer**. The village takes its name from the hammers that were once used in the iron forge that stood next to the River Tillingbourne. Stop at the T-junction and, before turning right, look left for the **Abinger Hammer Clock**, which shows a figure known as Jack the Hammer. On the hour, his hammer will strike the adjacent bell. You will need to ride a little way down the A25, but be alert as you will be taking the first left turning you come to. Follow this road until you see a gate up a ramp in front of you. To the left of this ramp is NCN22 but, being more like a footpath than a cycleway, it is easy to miss. Please be mindful of the walkers who use this route as well. Follow the trail until you reach a T-junction. Turn right here and you will now be on Wonham Way. At the T-junction, turn left to find yourself on the A25 once again. Once you pass under the bridge, you will see a sign for Gomshall Station. Turn right here and follow Station Approach until you see the station and the end of the journey.

EXTENSION: FRIDAY STREET AND THE WATERFALL

From Leith Hill Road, if you continue along Hollow Lane, at the first right turn you will see a sign for Friday Street. Turn right here and follow the single-track road as it slopes downwards. When you reach the bottom of the slope, you will see a pond which is all that remains of the mill that was once on this site. As you pass the pond, this becomes Noons Corner Road. Follow this road until you reach the junction and turn left, following the signpost to Wotton. Take the next right on to Broadmoor

Road. You will soon be directed to turn left but at this point you will need to walk: this is private land and bikes are prohibited. It is not a long walk and you will take a left turn. Look to your right as a couple of areas have been cleared to give you a view of the largest waterfall in Surrey. It is advisable to go there when there has been a lot of rain: when I visited, there was not a lot of water coming down. Go back the way you came to rejoin the route.

↑ The Tillingbourne Waterfall near Friday Street (Full Send Photography/S)

THE ESSENTIALS

GETTING THERE By train, the journey from London Waterloo is 1 hour, but you do need to change trains at Guildford. By car, Gomshall Station is 13km from the A3 when you come off at Guildford. There is a free car park next to the station but a sign does state that it is intended for people who are catching a train.

FACILITIES There are no public toilets on this ride.

WHERE TO EAT

Albert's Coffee Bar, Vintage Frog, 56 Station Rd, Gomshall, GU5 9LR; ☏ 01483 351020; ⌚ vintagefrog.co.uk; closed Mon. Located in the garden of the Vintage Frog antique shop, this is a good stop-off point at the start or the end of your ride. Teas, coffees, soft drinks and a selection of cakes are available. **£**

The Royal Oak, Felday Glade, Holmbury St Mary, RH5 6PF; ☏ 01306 898010; ⌚ theroyaloakholmbury.co.uk. The building dates to the 1730s and has been a pub since the mid-19th century. It serves main meals, sandwiches (lunchtime only) and light bites; you also have the bonus of the Felday Brewery on site for some very local beer (⌚ feldaybrewery.co.uk). **£–££**

Heartwork Coffee Bar, Bulmer Farm, Holmbury St Mary, RH5 6LG; ⌚ heartworkcoffee.co.uk. Serves a selection of light bites as well as a wide choice of coffees, teas and smoothies (I really liked the açai berry one), and soft drinks. **£**

13 HORSLEY TO EFFINGHAM JUNCTION

START	Horsley Railway Station
FINISH	Effingham Junction Railway Station
DISTANCE/TIME	27.8km/2¾hrs (extension: 2.3km 10mins)
DIFFICULTY/TERRAIN	② Flat for most of the ride but with some challenging off-road climbs; you will cross some A-roads and ride along B-roads and country lanes
SCENIC RATING	⑧ Forestry woodland with off-road cycling and occasional challenging rolling terrain on commons and heathland
SUITABLE FOR	MTB, gravel or sturdy hybrid (with off-road tyres)
CYCLE ROUTE	Surrey Cycleway, NCN22
MAPS	OS Explorer 145 and 146 (1:25 000)
KOMOOT REF	879067036

East Horsley was once part of the estate belonging to Lord Lovelace, and you will see evidence of the family while travelling through tree-lined lanes and past historic churches. You will ride across a vineyard and see four spectacular views showing Surrey at its finest. A feast of both stately homes and protected natural areas.

THE ROUTE

Exiting ❶ **Horsley Railway Station**, ride down Station Approach until you reach the T-junction. Turn left on to Ockham Road South (B2039). After riding for 1.5km, note a parade of shops on your left. Just beyond this is a distinctive building which is the entrance to **Horsley Towers**, a 19th-century country house that was once the home of William King, the Earl of Lovelace, and his wife Ada (see box, page 144). It is well worth making a quick detour here to have a look at this rather impressive edifice. The entrance building and some of the towers were built in the Lovelace style, which is a combination of flint and moulded white, black and red terracotta brick. The tower to the side is a fine example of this, and, because the village was once part of the estate owned by Lord Lovelace, there are several other buildings in East Horsley displaying this distinctive style.

← Horsley Towers (Ross Hamilton)

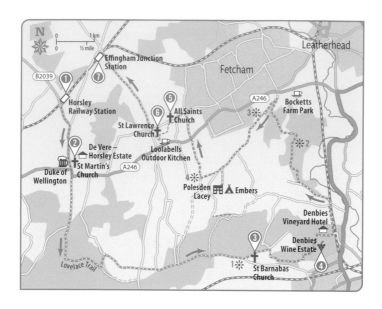

Just beyond Horsley Towers on the same side of the road is ❷ **St Martin's Church**. The tower is believed to be the oldest part of this church, dating back to the Saxon era. The remainder of the church dates to the Norman period and, like so many other churches in Surrey, it was restored in the Victorian era. There are a few features worth looking at, none more so than the tomb of Thomas Cornwallis – a member of Elizabeth I's court – and his wife Katherine. In the churchyard are two buildings constructed to Lord Lovelace's specifications. The first is a gazebo, where a choirboy was said to have been posted to warn the rector of the lord's arrival so the church service could start. The second is the Lovelace family mausoleum, which is open on certain days of the year (contact the church directly to find out when; ⌂ easthorsleychurch.org.uk).

At the T-junction, you will see another building in the Lovelace style: **Guildford Lodge**, once the entrance to Horsley Towers. Turn left on to Epsom Road (A246) and then right on to Chalk Lane, a single-track road. Follow this gentle climb for 1.2km; at the T-junction, turn right on to Green Dene. On your right is part of the **Sheepleas**, an area of ancient woodland owned by Surrey County Council. Areas of chalk grassland on this reserve, managed by Surrey Wildlife Trust, are home to 30 species of butterflies (including the brown argus) and plants such as bluebells, orchids and wild marjoram. After 120m, the road bears around to the right but you need stay to the left of the wooden fence to follow the trail called Honeysuckle Bottom (/// hurt.broker.stray).

You are now entering an area called the **Lovelace Bridges Trail**, which was built by the Lovelaces to transport timber around their estate by horse-drawn cart. Of the 15 bridges that were built, only ten remain and not all of them are accessible as they are now on private land. On this ride you will be passing under the Troye and Hermitage bridges. After 1km, take a sharp left on to Sheepwalk Lane. From here until you go under the second bridge you will have a continuous climb. The route flattens out after the bridge; then, take the first left turn. Follow the trail until you reach the T-junction and turn right on to Crocknorth Road which is part of the Surrey Cycleway. You will be on this undulating piece of road for 4km, although, after the crossroads, the road is called Ranmore Common Road. Just before you turn off this road, there is a car park on your right. You are at Denbies Hillside, which is a worthwhile stopping point to catch the first panoramic view of Surrey's beautiful countryside (/// wasp.claps.corner).

Turn left on to North Downs Way and you will soon see ❸ **St Barnabas Church**. Compared to most of the churches in this book, this is quite modern, having been built in the 1850s; it has an unusual feature in that the main door does not face the road. If the church is open, check out the Cubitt Chapel, which was constructed on the wishes of Henry Cubitt (Lord Ashcombe) to commemorate his three sons, all of whom died fighting in World War I. In the churchyard, look out for the gravestone which is a large cross entwined with an anchor.

Continue along the road until you reach a crossroads. Go straight over, passing by the white gate and the 'Private Road' sign. Just after the sign, take a right and stay on this track for 500m. This track is uneven, although you will soon come to a paved road. Do not join the road but stay on the

ADA KING: COUNTESS OF LOVELACE (1815–52)

Ada was the daughter of Lord Byron and mathematician Isabella Byron. She was introduced to Charles Babbage, who is today seen as the father of the computer thanks to his 'Difference Engine' (a mechanical calculator) and, later, his 'Analytical Machine' (essentially, a fully programmable computer with attached printer). Ada, an accomplished mathematician, published an algorithm for the machine showing how it could compute numbers, which means she is now regarded as the first computer programmer. The computer language 'Ada' is named in her honour.

track. This fast downhill track is quite narrow and can be muddy. Go through a wooden gate on your left and you will be on the ❹ **Denbies Wine Estate**. Do not deviate from this trail as this is one of the few routes through here on which cycling is permitted. After 550m, the track takes a sharp left and then a right. Ride on and turn right at the T-junction and ahead of you, on the horizon, is **Box Hill**. Follow the trail as it turns left and, when you arrive at the buildings, turn right. Here, you will see the **Denbies Vineyards Hotel**, wine shop, café, a farm shop and, if you go around the back of the building, the Surrey Hills Brewery.

Ride out of the estate but, before you reach the London Road (A24), take a left on to the cycle lane which is part of the Surrey Cycleway and NCN22. Follow this for 600m before turning left on to Westhumble Street, which is also part of Ride 15 (page 156). You will be on this road for 450m but, just before you reach Box Hill and Westhumble Station, look right to see two blue plaques to James and Susi Jeans. He was a noted physicist

↑ Ada Lovelace in a daguerreotype by Antoine Claudet, c1850 (The RedBurn/WC)

who made several discoveries (eg: Jeans Mass and Jeans Length) and she a musicologist, performer and music teacher.

At a gate with the word 'Leladene' carved into it is another blue plaque, this one celebrating novelist Fanny Burney, author of *Evelina*, the story of how a young lady navigates her way through Georgian society. Turn right on to Crabtree Lane and you will immediately see **The Chapel of Ease** on your right. The building might look like an old barn because it most probably was. After 750m, turn right on to the trail and you are now in **Norbury Park**. This is one of the better-paved tracks I have cycled on, but you will be travelling uphill for the next 1.75km. There are several speed bumps along here and, when the track levels out, make sure you stop around here and look to your right to catch the second wonderful view of Surrey on this ride. After you pass a gate, turn left at the area with the picnic benches in it (/// tests.heat.entry).

The land around **Norbury Park House** (which is behind the green fence you have just ridden past) was purchased by Surrey County Council to protect it from development. A wide variety of flora and fauna populate the park but please stick to the designated route so as not to disturb any of it, which includes all three native British woodpeckers. You will be riding mostly downhill for the next 1.4km. Follow the track as it bears left, and you will go past another gate. You will soon reach another and, once you are past this, bear right. You need to take a sharp left turn when you reach two metal gates on either side of the track (/// voted.next.mess). This is called Admirals Road. Cycle through the tunnel of trees for 600m; when the treeline stops, stand next to the signpost to your right and look back the way you came. This is the third excellent view on this journey: some of the taller buildings of London are clearly visible on the horizon (/// noises.owls.beats).

Continue along Admirals Road for a further 1.3km. This is not as well paved as the previous tracks and can be quite muddy. When you reach the road, go straight ahead and on to Polesden Road. After 600m, there is a sign for Polesden Lacey (see extension below). Take a right at this sign and, when the road forks, take the right-hand lane. The track becomes muddy but watch out – I have seen dirt bikers riding here. After 500m, you will need to turn right, but pause again here for a moment (/// gallons.

empire.flown). This is the fourth wonderful view on this ride. Take the right turn on to Chalkpit Lane. The track goes downhill for 1.2km but, be warned, it's quite worn in places. I have found it easier to stick to the left-hand side of this track.

At the end of Chalkpit Lane is the busy Guildford Road (A246). Take a right and then a quick left on to Rectory Lane. At the roundabout, turn left on to Lower Road. You can also ride on the pavement as it is a cycle lane. Turn left on to Manorhouse Lane. When you reach the end of the hedgerow, turn right up the path and you will soon come to ❺ **All Saints Church**. It is unclear when this secluded church was built but it is believed that it dates to the 1100s. It could well have been a manorial church of the local landowner, which might explain why it is so small. There is a rather impressive yew tree in the churchyard which is believed to be 1,300 years old.

Follow the path for another 300m and then take the middle path when it splits into three. Continue along into the King George V Playing Fields, which is also the home of Effingham and Leatherhead Rugby Club. Pass by Loolabells Outdoor Kitchen (see below) and leave the grounds, turning right on to Browns Lane. On your right, you will see ❻ **St Lawrence Church** with, in its churchyard, the gravestone of Barnes Wallis, inventor of the bouncing bomb (among other things). The church itself was built around 1100, having undergone restoration in 1888. If you look on the north wall, which is considered the earliest part of the church, you'll see a carved head staring out at you. This is thought to be the face of a prior, as this church was once owned by Merton Priory.

As you reach the church, the road becomes Church Street. At the T-junction, turn left on to Lower Road and then right at the first roundabout and right again at the next one. You now have a 2.5km ride up Effingham Common Road to ❼ **Effingham Junction Station** and the end of the ride.

EXTENSION: POLESDEN LACEY

Taking a left at the sign for **Polesden Lacey**, ride for 500m towards the estate. Now owned by the National Trust, it has 650ha of land in the Surrey Hills for you to explore. In the early 1900s the house was owned by the

Greville family who employed the architects of The Ritz hotel to redesign the interiors. This must have done the job, because in 1923 the future George VI and his wife Elizabeth spent part of their honeymoon here. Go to the website to see the summer events programme (⌖ nationaltrust. org.uk).

THE ESSENTIALS

GETTING THERE By train, Horsley Station is 50 minutes from London Waterloo and one stop along from Effingham Junction. By car, the station is 4.6km from the A3 (Ockham Park Junction) along Ockham Road North (B2039).

FACILITIES AND FURTHER INFORMATION Public toilets can be found next to Ryka's Cafe (Box Hill). **Visit Leatherhead** (⌖ visitleatherhead. com) is a web-only resource with information on things to do, places to explore, local events and transport links.

WHERE TO EAT

Duke of Wellington, Guildford Rd, East Horsley, KT24 6AA; ✆ 01483 282312; ⌖ dukeofwellingtoneasthorsley.co.uk. This old coaching inn serves lunch and evening meals all week. A cold breeze is said to blow near the fireplace at 18.00 most days, no matter how hot it is in the rest of the pub. It is believed to be a ghost of a lady known only as 'Irene'. **£–££**

Bocketts Farm Park, Young St, Fetcham, KT22 9BS; ✆ 01372 363764; ⌖ bockettsfarm.co.uk. This is an educational farm but you can visit the tearooms without entering the visitor attraction. A wide selection of food is available in the lovely setting of an 18th-century barn. Toilets are on site as well. **£**

Loolabells Outdoor Kitchen, King George V Playing Fields, Effingham, KT24 5ND; ✆ 07775 741555. Breakfast and lunch menu with sandwiches, baps, baguettes and burgers available. Hot and cold drinks too. The Melon Refresher smoothie did live up to its name. **£**

14 OCKLEY TO HOLMWOOD

START	Ockley Railway Station
FINISH	Holmwood Railway Station
DISTANCE/TIME	28.5km/2½hrs
DIFFICULTY/TERRAIN	② B-roads, country lanes and paved off-road paths; the big climb up Leith Hill is challenging
SCENIC RATING	⑧ Magnificent views from Leith Hill; villages, historic churches and lovely country pubs
SUITABLE FOR	MTB, gravel, hybrid or road bike
CYCLE ROUTE	Surrey Cycleway
MAPS	OS Explorer 146 and OL34 (1:25 000)
KOMOOT REF	909171122

T his ride takes you along some of the best country roads that Surrey has to offer. There are several churches to visit, a historic house once home to a great British composer, a sculpture park and some lovely pubs. There is a climb up Leith Hill, the highest point in Surrey, from which there are three wonderful views.

THE ROUTE

Coming out of ❶ **Ockley Station**, ride down to the end of Station Approach and turn right on to Coles Lane (B2126). Follow the road as it bears around to the right, past Village Greens Farm Shop (which is on your left). The road then bears to the left, and on your right you encounter ❷ **St Margaret's Church, Ockley**, founded in the late 13th century.

At the churchyard gate, there is a small stone wall to the right. On the other side, however, that is not actually a wall: it's a set of steps called a mounting block, which would have been used by parishioners to mount their horse after the service – and it may well have served riders of penny-farthings. Inside is a wooden plaque commemorating Henry Whitfield, Rector of the church between 1618 and 1638, who then left to sail to New England where he founded the settlement of Guildford in Massachusetts. His American house is still standing – the oldest stone structure in New England. Look out for the brief but informative guide to walking around the church.

Once you leave the church, turn left to come back the way you came along Coles Lane until you reach Weare Street on your right: you will follow this road for nearly 5km. It's part of the Surrey Cycleway and – apart from a stretch that would benefit from repairs to the surface – a lovely route to ride. After 1.5km, there is a pond on your left. A bench has been placed on its bank and it is a nice place to sit and just relax (/// wriggle. trials.buzzards).

At the end of Weare Street, you need to cross Bognor Road (A29) and continue along Ruckmans Lane. Very soon, the treeline on your right will have cleared, and I recommend you stop here to admire the view (/// mailboxes.bunk.earplugs). On a clear day, you can see the tower atop Leith Hill. Continue along Ruckmans Lane and, when the road bears to the right, look to another road leading off to the left passing the gap in a

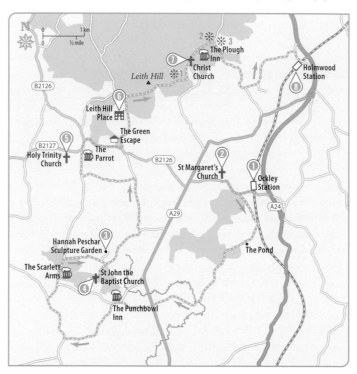

low wall. You are now crossing over the remains of **Stane Street**, a Roman road (see box, page 152). The road on your left follows its route. The parts of the road that would have been on your right have long disappeared.

When you arrive at a T-junction, turn left; you are still on Ruckmans Lane. On your left are a red post box and a red telephone box. The latter is now used by the village of **Okewood** (which you are on the outskirts of) as a community noticeboard. Keep pedalling and on your right is **The Punchbowl Inn** (see below); Okewood Cricket Club is behind the hedge on your left. A sign warns of cricket balls flying in this direction when a match is being played. Follow the road as it bears left; you are now on Honeywood Lane.

Some 2km after passing The Punchbowl Inn, you will reach a T-junction. Turn right here on to Horsham Road. After 1.2km, take a right following the sign for the Surrey Cycleway. Confusingly, the road you have left and the one you are entering are both called Horsham Road. As you come to **Walliswood**, look to your left as you pass the village's pub, **The Scarlett Arms** (see below): you will see a green with a small structure on it. If you walk up to inspect it, you'll see a rusting piece of machinery inside. A local resident I spoke to believed that this was once the village well, but it had not been used in her lifetime and she had been there for over 40 years.

Continue along Horsham Road and, 350m after the pub, take a right on to Standon Lane, at which point you leave the Surrey Cycleway. Standon Lane mostly slopes downwards, and it is easy to pick up a good deal of speed. However, be careful: there is a sharp left and a sharp right as you make you way down here. Keep your eyes peeled to your left after these turns for the ❸ **Hannah Peschar Sculpture Garden** (⌀ hannahpescharsculpture.com). Originally part of a large estate, the garden was restored by Hannah Peschar and her partner, and she curated the sculpture park for more than 40 years before retiring in 2015. Take care if you cycle down the entrance path as it is made up of loose stones and can prove challenging, especially on slick tyres.

Further along Standon Lane the road forks; turn right to follow Church Lane until you reach ❹ **St John the Baptist Church, Okewood**. The church was built in the 13th century but has had regular restoration work since

STANE STREET

Built by the Romans to link their port at Chichester with London, the name used for it today is not Roman at all. It is an old spelling of the word 'stone', which in turn was based on the Old English word *stan*. What the Romans called it is unknown. The original road was 91km long and it is believed to have been constructed in the first decade after Britain was first occupied, ie: some time between 43 and 53AD. The road had to wait until the 20th century before anyone decided to study it in depth; even though a good deal of the route has been discovered, some parts, especially through Dorking, remain a mystery. Some modern thoroughfares have been built on the route of this 2,000-year-old road. Look at a map of Ockley village, for example: the A29 which passes directly through the village is not only straight, as Roman roads generally were, but it is also called Stane Street.

the 1700s. Notable features include a brass located in the floor of the old chancel showing a soldier in full armour with a dedication to Edward de la Hale, Esquire to the County of Surrey. There are also the remains of some original paintings on the south wall of the chancel, but it is difficult to make out exactly what they depict.

Retrace your steps along Church Lane and turn right at the junction to rejoin Standon Lane. After 1.3km it becomes Mole Street and, after another 1.6km, take a left turning on to a road that does not seem to have a name. The road surface is quite poor in places, but it was still manageable, even on a road bike. After 1.3km, you will come to a gate, which you go through and turn right to rejoin Horsham Road and the Surrey Cycleway.

At the village of **Forest Green**, The Parrot pub will be on your right (see below). At the T-junction, turn left on to Ockley Road (B2127), where you will immediately see two buildings on your right. The left-hand building, dating to the 16th century, is a working **forge**, creating ironwork and continuing a tradition that was once prevalent in this area of Surrey (⊘ forestgreenforge.co.uk). A little further down the road, take a left at the sign pointing towards a church, which is not easy to see from the road, being surrounded by trees. This is ❺ **Holy Trinity Church** and it owes its construction to a tragedy. In 1892, Charles and Christina Hensley lost their eldest son, Everard, and had the church built in his memory. The five stained-glass windows in the east wall depict members of the Hensley family and their cousins, the Burneys. Everard is commemorated in the window on the far right.

Come out of the church and, at first retracing your steps, turn right back on to Ockley Road (B2127). Follow the road around to the left and to the right. The right bend marks the point where, although still called Ockley Road, it becomes the B2126. You will also notice it climbing steadily upwards, which will continue for the next 2.4km. That is because you are making your way up **Leith Hill**, the highest point in Surrey. You will not be going all the way to the summit, but you will be following part of the route that was used by the Prudential RideLondon.

You will come to a set of road signs, including a brown National Trust one pointing towards Leith Hill. Turn left here and on to Leith Hill Lane. When you see a high brick wall on your right, you will be near the end of the most challenging part of the climb; quite quickly there will also be a wall on your left. This is ❻ **Leith Hill Place**, a 17th-century house which was the home of Josiah Wedgewood III of the pottery family. His grandson was the composer Vaughan Williams (famous for his piece

↑ 'Sound Architecture 5.0', by Ronald van der Meijs at the Hannah Peschar Sculpture Garden, is comprised of 5,000 chromed bicycle bells (Ronald van der Meijs/WC)

'The Lark Ascending'), who lived here as a child. The house is currently closed but due to reopen in 2024. You will pass a couple more buildings before you need to turn right on to Abinger Road. All that climbing is worth it, because there eventually comes a break in the trees and you will have the first of the great views that Leith Hill has to offer, looking back at the area you were riding through earlier (/// acute.crust.issue).

After 2km on Abinger Road, you will arrive at ❼ **Christ Church, Coldharbour**, a church dating only to 1848 but looking much older. There is a Vaughan Williams connection: his sister paid for the organ to be restored in 1932. One of the stained-glass windows depicts a monk with a ray of sunshine on him; it was designed by Hugh Easton, who was responsible for the Battle of Britain Memorial Window in Westminster Abbey. Head upstairs to see the displays telling the history of the church. The churchyard contains the graves of Marian and Caja Hemar: he was a Polish entertainer who broadcast from England to Poland during the German Occupation in World War II; she was an actor who, before she settled in England, lived in the USA. She is believed to be one of the models holding the torch aloft at the start of Columbia Pictures movies.

As you continue along Abinger Road, you will come to the village of Coldharbour, the highest community in the south of England. This is a great place to rest up, especially if you fancy popping into The Plough Inn and its shop (see *Accommodation*, page 227). The pub is also home to the Leith Hill Microbrewery: Smiler's Happiness Pale Ale is worth a try. The shop sells some bike spares and has a pump. It also sells a range of hot and cold food. Seating is available at the back of the pub.

Continue to the end of Abinger Road, but before you turn right, stop here and look left for the second of the great views (/// joke.bink.roses). The red telephone box contains a Park Tool Outdoor Tool Station, which includes Allen keys and tyre levers. Turn right on to Anstie Lane where on the left is Anstiebury Farm; if you walk over to the right-hand gate, the third great view is visible in all its glory (/// enable.pinks.often). If you look hard enough, you can see planes taking off and landing at Gatwick Airport.

For the next 1.5km, you will be travelling downhill. You can pick up a good deal of speed here, but this is a single-track road so be aware of vehicles coming the other way and some tight bends. Liberal use of brakes is advised on this descent. You should see some white gates and a sign to Trout Grange. This could be the trickiest piece of track for a road bike, especially in the winter as some of it is not well paved and can be muddy in places. You will come to a metal gate (/// skinny.dishes.sofa). Pass through here and you are now on Moorhurst Lane, which you follow until you come to the T-junction. Turn right and you will be on Old Horsham Road. After 250m, you will reach a bridge and see signs for your destination, ❽ **Holmwood Station**.

THE ESSENTIALS

GETTING THERE By train, the journey from London Victoria to Ockley is 1 hour and 10 minutes. By car, Ockley Station is just off the A24, 10.5km from Dorking in the north and 11km from Horsham in the south. There is a pay-and-display car park next to the station.

FACILITIES There are no public toilets on this ride.

WHERE TO EAT

The Punchbowl Inn, Okewood Hill, Ockley, RH5 5PU; ☏ 01306 627249; ⌂ punchbowlinnokewoodhill.com. This old village pub dates to the 16th century and is beautiful inside and out. Main meals are always available; sandwiches at lunchtimes only. See their website for kitchen opening hours. They have a little shop on site, located in what used to be the pub's stables, which sells snacks and drinks to take away. £–££

The Scarlett Arms, Horsham Rd, Walliswood, RH5 5RD; ☏ 01306 627243; ⌂ scarlettarms. co.uk. The building dates to the 1600s when it was two cottages, but it has been a pub since 1907. Serves main meals, light bites and sandwiches (lunchtime only). I highly recommended the BLT. Kitchen closed on Mon & Tues. £–££

The Parrot, Horsham Rd, Forest Green, RH5 5RZ; ☏ 01306 775790; ⌂ brunningandprice. co.uk/parrot. This has been a pub since 1712; there is a brief history on the website. Specialising in main meals, it can also offer starters and a steak sandwich if you want something lighter. If you go on the right day in the summer, you can sit in the garden and watch the cricket on the other side of the road. £–£££

15 BOX HILL AND WESTHUMBLE TO CLAYGATE

START/	Boxhill and Westhumble Railway Station
FINISH	Claygate Railway Station
DISTANCE/TIME	22.1km/2hrs
DIFFICULTY/TERRAIN	① Paved roads with a moderate climb for the first 5km; mostly downhill after that following cycle routes and country lanes; there is a crossing over a busy A-road; 25% is off-road
SCENIC RATING	Ⓐ Woodland areas of Ashtead Common and Prince's Coverts, Langley Vales Woods World War I Memorial as well as the historic village of Headley
SUITABLE FOR	MTB, gravel or sturdy hybrid (with off-road tyres)
CYCLE ROUTE	NCN22, Surrey Cycleway
MAPS	OS Explorer 146 and 161 (1:25 000)
KOMOOT REF	1017069362

Box Hill takes its name from the boxwood plant that grows there, and you may see some while travelling along the peaceful country roads nearby. You will pass through the village of Headley, the wildlife-rich Ashtead Common, and Langley Vale Woods (with its World War I memorial), before finishing off at arguably the smallest pub in the UK.

THE ROUTE

We start at the lovely ❶ **Box Hill and Westhumble Station**. The railway line was built here in the mid-1800s and passes through Norbury Park, which was owned at the time by Thomas Grissell (see Ride 13, page 145). In compensation for the railway passing through his estate, he asked for a station to be built (like Lord Thurlow; see Ride 8, page 98). The station is now Grade II-listed and it is easy to see why. With a lick of paint and some appropriate signage, it would not look out of place in a period drama. Out of the station, turn right on to Westhumble Street. Passing The Stepping Stones pub, you will soon see the A24 (London Road). On your left is a sign for the Surrey Cycle Link (NCN22) and 'Cyclists Dismount' is written

← The 'Regiment of Trees' at Langley Vale Wood (Mertbiol/WC)

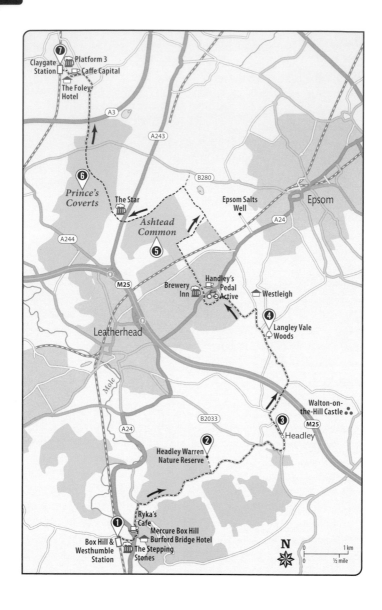

Claygate Station
Platform 3
Caffe Capital
The Foley Hotel
A3
A243
7

Prince's Coverts
6
B280
The Star
Epsom Salts Well
Epsom
A24
A244
Ashtead Common
5

M25
Brewery Inn
Handley's Pedal Active
Westleigh
Langley Vale Woods
4

Leatherhead

Mole

Walton-on-the-Hill Castle
B2033
A24
Headley Warren Nature Reserve
2
3
M25
Headley

Ryka's Cafe
1
Mercure Box Hill
Burford Bridge Hotel
Box Hill & Westhumble Station
The Stepping Stones

N

0   1 km
0   ½ mile

on the path. Follow this path and continue through the underpass. When you come out, turn left and follow the cycle track/pavement up and over the bridge which crosses the River Mole.

Follow the cycle path and turn right on to Old London Road (B2209). **Box Hill**, on your right, has been a popular cycle route since the late 1880s. Continue along this road for 800m and turn right on to Headley Lane. You will be riding along here for 3.5km. Headley Lane is designated an Area of Outstanding Natural Beauty and is a joy to ride; at times it is quiet enough to hear the birds singing. Headley Lane changes to Lodgebottom Road just before you see Cockshott Car Park on your left. Just behind the car park is the ❷ **Headley Warren Nature Reserve**, which looks stunning in the spring when the ground is covered in bluebells.

The road slopes gently upwards and you reach a T-junction. Turn right on to Leech Lane (B2033) and, after 650m, turn left on to Nut Ash Lane. Take the next left on to Church Lane and make your way to the village of ❸ **Headley**. Mentioned in the Domesday Book, Headley was once owned by Countess Goda, sister of Edward the Confessor. Headley Village Stores is cycle-friendly and a nice stop-off point for a drink. Sandwiches are available at the weekend (closed Mon). Next door is The Cock Inn and behind that the church of St Mary the Virgin. The current church was completed in 1859 but records show buildings here from as early as 1311. A grotto outside the church houses the font that was once inside before the 1859 rebuild. The church is quite big for a village of this size and there are coffee-and-cake mornings on a Friday

↑ Church of St Mary the Virgin in Headley (Dr Neil Clifton/WC)

Continue along Church Lane, rejoining NCN22, and turn right on to Hurst Lane. Cycle down here for 2km, passing under the M25, and veering to the left as it becomes Walton Road. Turn right on to Headley Road, joining the Surrey Cycleway. You will see a car park on your right, which is the entrance to ❹ **Langley Vale Wood**. During World War I, this site was used as an army training camp and now houses a memorial to the conflict. Known as 'The Regiment of Trees', it consists of 12 carved soldiers, commemorating Lord Kitchener's visit here during the war to inspect the troops. The site is also home to a significant number of flora (such as bluebells and early purple orchid) and fauna (including birds such as the skylark and lapwing).

Continue straight on at the crossroads and cycle along Farm Lane. Take the first left on to Park Lane to enter Ashtead, and continue along there until turning left on to Dene Road. The road bears around to the right and becomes Rectory Lane. Be careful at this turn because it is tight and almost a blind corner: stay as close to the left as possible to avoid oncoming traffic. Near the end of Rectory Lane is Pedal Active (see *Cycle Hire and Repairs*, page 230): a useful stop-off point if your bike needs a quick service, or if you need cycling accessories. They even offer a sports massage! Booking in advance is advisable for both services.

At the end of Rectory Lane is a pub with one of the more unusual names I have come across: The Leg of Mutton and Cauliflower. Where the name comes from is a bit of a mystery, but it might have something to do with the crops that were once grown in the area. You need to turn right on to The Street (A24) but be careful as this road can be quite busy. Take an immediate left on to Woodfield Lane, passing the Brewery Inn on the corner. Follow Woodfield Lane for 870m, passing by Ashtead Village Pond on your left. At the roundabout, turn right and then immediately left. Continue down Woodfield Lane, passing over the level crossing at Ashtead Station and on to Bridleway 33. You are now entering ❺ **Ashtead Common**.

A Site of Special Scientific Interest, Ashtead Common is owned and managed by the City of London Corporation. It is home to butterflies such as the purple hairstreak, mammals such as the serotine bat, and birds such as the tawny owl and the green woodpecker. At the entrance to

COAL-TAX POSTS

Coal-tax posts were erected by the City of London Corporation approximately 25km from the now demolished General Post Office in St Martin's Le Grand in London. You can see the corporation logo on the posts: a white shield with a red cross and sword. Taxes have been placed on coal coming into the city since the Middle Ages and the posts were designed to show the boundary of the taxable area. The tax was never popular: most people who paid it saw no benefit because the majority of the money was spent in the City itself. Most of the posts you will see are white pillars measuring 1m in height, with another 1m beneath the ground. At least 200 are still *in situ*, and they can be found besides roads and tracks

the common, you will see a map, on which you will notice on the eastern edges of the common an area called **The Wells**. If you fancy a little detour, you will find the well in which Epsom Salts were originally sourced. The route bears to the right: continue until you reach a sign for Bridleway 38. Turn left and ride along here until you reach the signpost for Bridleway 29. Turn left, passing the coal-tax post (see box above). Stay on Bridleway 29 for 1.5km until you reach Kingston Road (A243).

Turn right on to the A243 then make an almost immediate left just before The Star pub, to cycle along The Avenue. Once you pass through

↑ A coal-tax post on Arbrooke Common in Claygate (Colin Smith/WC)

the gate, you will be on ❻ **Prince's Coverts**, an area of managed woodland owned by the Crown Estates. It acquired its name because it was once owned by King Leopold I of Belgium when he was still a prince. He lived at Claremont Park in Esher in the early 1800s and bought this land to partake in shooting the local wildlife. After his death, the land was purchased by the British royal family and has been part of the Crown Estates ever since. Follow this route for 1.5km until you come to another gate. Pass through this and cross over Fairoak Lane (B280). This part of the ride can be very muddy. Cross a bridge over the A3 (Esher Bypass) and you will find yourself on the outskirts of Claygate.

Follow Coverts Road for about 700m until it bears to the left and becomes Church Road. The twin spires of Holy Trinity Church will appear on the skyline to your left. This impressive building dates from the Victorian era, but the interior has been modernised so, in my opinion, it is best viewed from the outside. At the end of Church Road, turn left at the first roundabout and left again at the second. You will now be on Hare Lane. Continue along this road for 450m. Turn left on to The Parade; at

↑ The Prince's Coverts (Hugh Craddock/WC)

the end of this road is your destination: **❼ Claygate Station**. Hopefully **Platform 3** is open when you arrive, because not only is this the smallest pub in the country (allegedly), but the owner is also a fellow cyclist and likes nothing more than to talk bikes while you enjoy his fine brews.

THE ESSENTIALS

GETTING THERE By train, Box Hill and Westhumble Station is a 47-minute journey from London Waterloo, or 56 minutes from London Victoria. To return from Claygate to Box Hill and Westhumble, change trains at Wimbledon. By car, the station is 8.5km from Junction 9 of the M25, along the A243 and the A24.

FACILITIES AND FURTHER INFORMATION Public toilets can be found next to Ryka's Cafe (Box Hill), Ashtead Memorial Hall Car Park and Ashtead Station. **Visit Leatherhead** (⊘ visitleatherhead.com) is a web-only resource with information on things to do, places to explore, local events and transport links.

WHERE TO EAT

Ryka's Cafe, Old London Rd, Dorking, RH5 6BY; ⊘ 01306 884454; ⊘ rykas.co.uk. Burgers, baguettes, baps, jacket potatoes and b/fasts. Ryka's has been a popular stop for bike riders of all varieties, serving since the 1920s. Open seven days a week. **£**

Handley's, 27 The Street, Ashtead, KT21 1AA; ⊘ 01372 279537; ⊘ handleyscafe. co.uk; closed Sun. Serving meals and light bites, this is a welcome stop halfway through the ride. **£**

Caffe Capital, 16 The Parade, Claygate, KT10 0NU; ⊘ caffecapital.co.uk/claygate. Light bites, hot & cold drinks as well as a full b/fast option. You can fill up your bike water bottle here for free. The menu is displayed on a retro peg-letter board, which is a nice touch. Open seven days a week. **£**

16 HOLMWOOD COMMON LOOP NORTH

START/FINISH	Fourwents Pond Car Park, Holmwood Common
DISTANCE/TIME	24.5km/2hrs (two extensions; 1: 3.91km, 30min round trip; 2: 5.5km, 40min round trip)
DIFFICULTY/TERRAIN	① Paved country roads and mostly flat with the occasional uphill
SCENIC RATING	④ Farmland, beautiful views, historic villages, churches and pubs; there is also a ruined castle (Extension 1)
SUITABLE FOR	MTB, gravel or hybrid
CYCLE ROUTE	Surrey Cycleway
MAPS	OS 146 Explorer (1:25 000)
KOMOOT REF	1150622655

↑ Fourwents Pond on Holmwood Common (John Miller/A)

T hroughout this ride, you will be riding along country roads with churches and pubs dating back over 500 years. You will also catch a glimpse of a windmill, a telephone box converted into an information kiosk, and a distillery as well as a brewery. There are opportunities on the extensions to see a ruined castle and to cycle round beautiful ancient woodland.

THE ROUTE

Starting at the ❶ **Fourwents Pond Car Park**, Mill Road, turn left on to Mill Road itself. At the T-junction, turn left on to Blackbrook Road. For most of this ride, the roads will be lined with high trees and hedges, but there is an occasional gap offering a nice view of the countryside. Take the next right on to Red Lane and stay on it for 2.3km, although 270m after you cross over the railway line it changes its name to Brockhamhurst Road. At the T-junction, turn right on to Leigh Road. When you pass over Gad Brook, this road also changes its name – to Shellwood Road. Turn left on to Bunce Common Road and stay on it for 2.1km.

Leigh Cricket Club is on your right and a sign for the village will appear on your left. **Leigh** (pronounced 'lie') has had some famous residents in its time, one of which being Donald Campbell, once the holder of both land and water speed records. You will see several pictures of him in **The Seven Stars** pub. The pub building dates to the 16th century, so be careful of the low ceilings. There is also quite a large fireplace, which does have a fire in it when the weather demands it. Follow the road as it bears to the right and becomes Tapner's Road.

On your right, you will see a small wooden building: this is a bus stop and one of the most attractive I have seen. Once you pass **The Plough** (see below), you will see another wooden structure which holds what used to be the village water pump. Turn left on to Church Road, joining the Surrey Cycleway. As you make your way along the road, you will see an old red telephone box which has been converted, as the sign at the top of it says, into a **'History Box'**: a wealth of interesting historical information about the village. This includes local wood being felled for Henry VIII's now lost Nonsuch Palace in Cheam; and in World War II the air raid siren essentially being a man ringing a bell while riding a bicycle.

❷ **St Bartholomew's Church** dates to the 1500s but went through a period of restoration during the Victorian era. All the stained glass dates from this time but look under the middle window in the south wall: it looks as though a smaller window was once here but has been bricked up. Look on the north wall for a memorial to Frederick Somes, a businessman who had links to the sea, a fact alluded to by the anchor. The churchyard contains a leaping board in remarkably good condition compared to others we have seen in this book (see Rides 3, page 51, and 8, page 97).

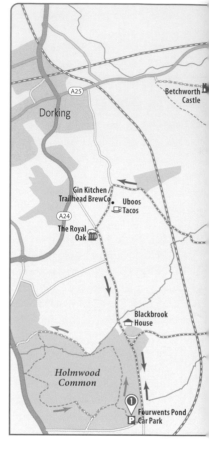

Continue along Church Road and at the T-junction turn right on to Flanchford Road, following the sign to Reigate. You will be going along this road for 1.6km but be careful when you cross over the River Mole at Flanchford Bridge as it is single-track. Take the next left to continue along Flanchford Road.

Look for the road marking indicating that the road is becoming single-track. It also starts to slope upwards, at which point you are no longer on the Surrey Cycleway. Ahead of you are two chevron signs; take the track in between them. Look over the top of the hedges on your right and you will see **Reigate Heath Windmill**. Located behind Reigate Golf Course Club House, the windmill stopped being a working mill many years ago and, since the 1880s, it has been used as a chapel.

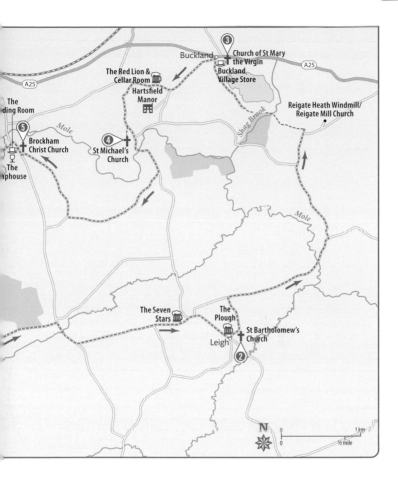

You need to plan your visits well in advance, though, as it is only open one Sunday a month during the summer.

Follow the track as it bears to the left but be mindful as a good many walkers also use this route. When you come to the stream, turn left. The track now becomes Dungates Lane, which you will follow for 1.2km. You will also pass over the stream, which is called Shag Brook

THE LEGEND OF SHAG BROOK

As you pass over Shag Brook, you are near a site that has become associated with some local legends. The first tells of a farmer's daughter who was taken to the side of the brook by the local landowner's son. The son is said to have made his intentions for the evening known in such a way that the girl died from the shock! Unable to live with what he had done, he committed suicide by stabbing himself through the heart. When the bodies were found, it is said that blood was trickling from a nearby stone, which would not stop no matter how much the stone was wiped.

The 'Bleeding Stone' is the focus of another legend: the Buckland Shag. This beast was said to sit on the stone around midnight. Horses would refuse to pass. And foolhardy visitors would bet the locals they could make it past the stone unharmed. One such visitor was a young soldier, drinking at an inn, who claimed he could ride from the inn to the stone and back. He made his way there without incident, but on the way back he felt an invisible arm grab him around the waist. He spurred the horse to gallop back to the inn, and only when he saw the building's lights did the frightful grip loosen. The area is said to be haunted by Shag no longer, as the Bleeding Stone was moved in the early 1800s by the lord of the manor to quell the fears of his tenants.

(see box above for the legends associated with it). When you come to the first set of buildings, the track becomes paved. When you reach the junction, look right. The white building is **Buckland Village Store** (see below).

The route from here turns left down Old Road, but you may wish to examine **Buckland** village before doing this. The ❸ **Church of St Mary the Virgin** dates to the 14th century and underwent major renovation in the Victorian era. I wasn't able to enter while researching this book as restoration work was being carried out on the organ and the building was locked at the time of writing, except for services. Across the road is the village pond; behind it you will see a building with an oxidised copper spire containing a bell. Now a private residence, this lovely building was once the village school.

Turn left on to Old Road and follow this for 1.2km. You will cycle past The Red Lion & Cellar Room (see *Accommodation*, page 228). Turn left on to The Street following the sign for Betchworth Church and Leigh. Take a right on to Church Street for ❹ **St Michael's Church**, the second church in this book used in the filming of *Four Weddings and a Funeral*. It is also a Grade I-listed building, with some parts dating back to the Saxon era. Look out for the banner of General Sir Charles Richardson, who had a distinguished military career in World War II. On the floor near his banner is a memorial to the Stables family. Edward, the first name on the list, died at the Battle of Waterloo, where his body still lies. Go back down Church Street and turn right on to The Street.

After you pass The Dolphin pub, the road changes name to Snowerhill Road and you are also back on the Surrey Cycleway. Look right and you will see a high brick wall, behind which is a taller building with a white clock tower atop it. This was once the home of Henry Goulburn who will be mentioned later. Just after a wooden carving, turn right on to Wellhouse Lane. The carving, representing a swirling seed, is the emblem of the Surrey Hills Area of Outstanding Natural Beauty. Take the next right turn on to Wheelers Lane which you will follow for 1.2km.

At the end of Wheelers Lane and on your right is ❺ **Brockham Christ Church**, a relatively recent build (1847) compared to others in this book. It was paid for by monies

↑ The emblem of the Surrey Hills Area of Outstanding Natural Beauty (Ross Hamilton)

raised by Henry Goulburn in memory of his son, also called Henry, who predeceased his father. Henry was an MP for nearly 50 years, representing five different constituencies and holding positions such as Chancellor of the Exchequer and Home Secretary. A memorial to him can be seen above the main entrance to the church.

At the junction, turn right on to Middle Street. You're now in **Brockham** village: its 5 November celebration includes a massive bonfire as well as a torchlight procession – an almost annual event for the best part of 80 years. In the distance, you will see some areas of exposed rock in the Surrey Hills, evidence of a once-thriving lime-works, the remains of which are still visible to this day.

Take the left turn after the old water pump, on to Tanner's Hill. You pass a right turn on to Coach Road which is the route to Betchworth Castle (see Extension 1 below). After passing that turn, the road changes name to Old School Lane (and, further on, Bushbury Lane). After 1.6km, turn right on to Parkpale Lane. Take the next right turn on to Tilehurst Lane which you will follow for 1.6km. There is a short climb after you have passed under the railway bridge. At the T-junction, turn left on to Punchbowl Lane. Look out for the first set of buildings you come to on your left. Here you will be able to pick up some food (Uboos Tacos; closed

↑ Brockham bonfire the day before being lit (Amanda Thompson)

Mon–Thu), some lovely beer (Trailhead BrewCo; closed Mon–Thu) and some equally lovely gin (The Gin Kitchen; closed Tue).

At the T-junction, turn left on to Chart Lane South. You'll be on this road for 2.7km. You will straight away pass The Royal Oak on your right; as you pass Inholms Lane, the road changes name to Blackbrook Road. Turn right on to Mill Road and then right again into the Fourwents Pond Car Park and the end of the ride. Those of you with some energy in reserve can try Extension 2 around Holmwood Common

EXTENSION 1: BETCHWORTH CASTLE

On this ride you can tick off another of Surrey's castles. To get here, turn right off Tanner's Hill in Brockham and on to Coach Road. Follow this road, which does have several pot-holes, for 1.4km. Turn right at the end of the track and look right for a footpath and a wooden gate.

↑ The ruins of Betchworth Castle (Ross Hamilton)

You will need to walk through the golf course but be mindful of your surroundings just in case a ball comes your way. The castle is at /// honey. farmer.camera. The original castle was possibly built on an Iron Age fort. It was rebuilt as a stone castle in the late 1300s and then became a fortified manor house less than a hundred years later. The site is now a ruin and, as you saw, surrounded by a golf course. To rejoin the main ride, come back the way you came.

EXTENSION 2: HOLMWOOD COMMON

Managed by the National Trust, Holmwood Common was once used by residents to graze livestock, collect firewood and fish. The grazing of animals had stopped by the 1950s, which allowed the trees and hedges to grow, giving us the wooded land we see today. There are numerous trails throughout the Common, most of which you are requested not to cycle on. However, there is a 5km circular route which you can follow, either clockwise or anticlockwise. There are several signs pointing the way but I would highly recommend using komoot to help you navigate. Start at Fourwents Mill Road Car Park and look out for the Little Ponds, Black Brook Ford, and the white horse's head pole, once used to tether animals. The map in the car park will give you an idea as to their location. There are 260ha of the Common in total, with ancient woodland, grassland and several ponds. You can see butterflies, dragonflies, deer and a variety of birds, including chiffchaffs, blackcaps and willow warblers.

↑ The horse's head pole on Holmwood Common (Ross Hamilton)

THE ESSENTIALS

GETTING THERE By train, the nearest stations to the start/finish point are Holmwood (2.55km; 1 hour 6 minutes from London Victoria) or Dorking (6.30km; 50 minutes from London Waterloo). By car, to get to Fourwents Pond Car Park (Holmwood Common), take the Mill Road exit off the Horsham Road (A24).

FACILITIES There are no public toilets on this ride.

WHERE TO EAT

The Plough, Church Rd, Leigh, RH2 8NJ; ✆ 01306 611348; ⊘ theploughleigh.co.uk. Dating from the 15th century (if not earlier), The Plough offers an extensive menu of main meals and light bites. Smaller sizes of some main meals are available for cyclists not wanting to load up too much. See the website for kitchen opening hours. **£–££**

Buckland Village Store, Dungates Lane, RH3 7BB; ✆ 01737 845999; ⊘ bucklandsurrey.net. Located in what could once have been a house (there is a fireplace *in situ*), you are offered a wide choice of bread and fillings. They also offer a selection of drinks as well as a small range of gifts and cards. **£**

The Reading Room Coffee and Cake House, Brockham Green, RH3 7JJ; ✆ 07514 833322; closed Mon. This lovely café has a wide selection of light bites and cakes as well as hot and cold drinks. This is quite a popular stop for cyclists passing through Brockham. If you fancy something a little stronger, around the back is The Tap House (⊘ taphousebrockham.co.uk), a bar that sells a variety of drinks as well as brewing its own beers. **£**

17 HOLMWOOD COMMON LOOP SOUTH

START/FINISH	Fourwents Pond Car Park, Holmwood Common
DISTANCE/TIME	24.5km/2hrs (extension: 7.2km round trip, 45mins)
DIFFICULTY/TERRAIN	① Paved country roads; mostly flat with the occasional uphill
SCENIC RATING	Ⓐ Farmland, a windmill, historic villages and their churches
SUITABLE FOR	MTB, gravel or sturdy hybrid
CYCLE ROUTE	Surrey Cycleway
MAPS	OS Explorer 146 (1:25 000)
KOMOOT REF	1154112347

This ride takes in some of the least populated areas of Surrey. Travelling along the border between Surrey and West Sussex, you will pass by several farms which means you get a real feel for the countryside (as well as some of the smells!). If you look closely, you will also find an 18th-century gaol. You can also cycle round an old brickworks that is now a nature reserve.

THE ROUTE

Starting at the ❶ **Fourwents Pond Car Park**, Mill Road, turn left on to Mill Road itself. At the T-junction, turn right on to Henfold Lane, which you will be following for 3.4km. As you pass the sign for the Henfold Lakes camping site, there is a short climb, which according to the road sign has a 17% upward gradient. When you come to the junction at the end of Henfold Lane, turn right on to Village Street. You are now entering **Newdigate**. As you continue down the road, look left and you will see Bob's Shop, the only store in the village. It is here that you turn right for the extension (see below). Further along Village Street and on your left is ❷ **St Peter's Church**.

The oldest parts of the church date to the 1200s but, like so many others in Surrey, it underwent major renovations in the Victorian era. One of its distinguishing features is its wooden tower. The timber has been dated to the early 1500s; only one other church in Surrey, in the village of Burstow, has a similar design. (Burstow is east of Gatwick

← The war memorial and Six Bells pub in Newdigate (Colin Smith/WC)

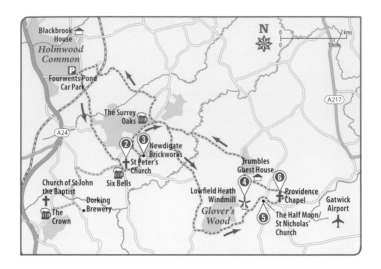

Airport but not included on any of the rides in this book.) The tower contains six bells, which is where the pub opposite (see below) gets its name from. Look out for the wonderful carved angels on the choir stalls. These, along with some other carvings in the church, date to the early 20th century and are examples of the work of a local resident who embarked on wood-carving classes.

Turn left on to Church Road and continue along here as it bears to the left, where it becomes Hogspudding Lane. The road slopes gently upwards and, on your right, you will see Mulberry Place. Turn right here and follow the road to the left where you will enter the car park to the ❸ **Newdigate Brickworks**. Clay was once excavated here for use in brickmaking; now production has stopped, the area has been converted into a nature reserve managed by the Surrey Wildlife Trust. The pits where the clay was dug have filled with water and, along with the woodland and grassland areas, are now home to a wide range of flora (blackthorn and dog rose) and fauna (crested newt). Cycling is allowed but only on the marked routes. To return to the ride, go back the way you came, turning right at the end of Mulberry Place and back on to Hogspudding Lane.

SURREY WILDLIFE TRUST

Throughout this guide, you have ridden across land managed by the Surrey Wildlife Trust. Its beginnings can be traced back to 1959 when a group of conservationists formed a society to protect and record Surrey's flora and fauna. The Trust has grown considerably since then, with a continuing mission to protect wildlife, and this includes several rare species living in what have become equally rare heathland habitats. It also aims to restore wetland and rivers. The Trust manages land for nature all over Surrey, not only on behalf of the County Council but other organisations such as the Ministry of Defence. It relies on volunteers, membership and donations to continue its work, details of which can be found on its website (⌀ surreywildlifetrust.org).

↑ The Surrey Wildlife Trust reserve at Newdigate Brickworks (Ross Hamilton)

At the T-junction, turn right on to Parkgate Road. After **The Surrey Oaks** pub on your left (see below), you will reach a left turn. Do not take it but note that this is where you will be turning off when you come back later in the ride. Continue straight and the road changes name, becoming Partridge Lane. It's mostly farms along this road, so buildings are sparse. Ride along Partridge Lane for 4.5km; just before you reach a T-junction, look left: you may see some llamas in the field.

Turn left on to Charlwood Lane and stay on it for 2.9km, although it changes its name to Russ Hill and then Rectory Lane. After 770m, keep an eye out to your left for a gate, which is the entrance to **Glover's Wood**. Managed by the Woodland Trust, it is a Site of Special Scientific Interest (SSSI) and the home of some rare species of plants and animals, such as the hawfinch, which, for unknown reasons, has become quite a rare bird in the UK.

This road is on the edge of the Surrey–West Sussex border and **Gatwick Airport** is just to the east, so your ride down this country road will be disturbed by the occasional plane flying parallel to you. There is a nice view of the airport where the road bears left at Russ Hill Farm, which has a distinctive Chinese dragon design on its gate. Further along this road, look left and you will see the ❹ **Lowfield Heath Windmill** (⊘ lowfieldheathwindmill. co.uk), one of the few to survive the move to steam-driven machinery. Once past the windmill, you will soon enter **Charlwood**, a historic village with over 80 listed buildings within its borders.

As the road bears to the right (with Charlwood Parish Hall on your left), it becomes The Street. After you pass Murray Designs (on your right), take the next right turning. This is also known as The Street, and you will soon see ❺ **The Half Moon** pub (see below), next door to which is **St Nicholas' Church**. Look out for one of the yew trees in the churchyard, which is almost hollow and looks as though it has been damaged by fire, yet still alive nonetheless. The church itself was built in 1080 and is Grade I-listed. It is worth visiting for its medieval wall painting, which depicts scenes from the lives of St Margaret, St Nicholas and St Edmund. There is a reconstruction of this painting on the left as you walk in, and an explanation of what is happening can be found under the originals.

When you come out of the church, follow The (smaller) Street to the left as this is a one-way road. At the T-junction on to The (larger) Street, turn right and look out for the village shop. Down Rosemary Lane, which runs beside it, is a small building called The Cage (there is a similar structure in the village of Lingfield: see Ride 19, page 199). Built circa 1792, this was once the local lock-up for the accused awaiting trial. Turn left down Chapel Road where the last building you will see is ❻ **Providence Chapel**. This was originally in nearby Horsham and was used as a barracks guardhouse during the Napoleonic Wars, it is now used by the local school. It can be visited by booking a time in advance (see ⌂ providencechapelcharlwood. org for details). From the Chapel, the road is not as well paved; at the end, you will reach a gate, which you pass through and turn left on to Pudding Lane. Pass through the next gate and, at the junction, cross over Norwood Hill Road and on to Stan Hill, which you will ride along for 2.6km. Look out for the road sign for Norwood Hill; once you pass this, you will be on the Surrey Cycleway, the road changes name to Blanks Lane not long

↑ The Half Moon pub and Church of St Nicholas in Charlwood (Amanda Thompson)

afterwards. At the T-junction, turn right and you will be back on Partridge Lane, albeit briefly.

Take the next right on to Broad Lane and then an almost immediate left on to Mill Lane. The surface is not well paved: look out for the numerous pot-holes. Turn left on to Ewood Lane, which you will follow for 1.8km. The sign says that this is a private road, but cyclists are permitted. The road turns into a track, which can be muddy, but not long after riding through a gate it improves. Take a left on to the concreted bridleway (Bridleway 224), pass underneath the railway bridge, and then turn left on to Lodge Lane. At the junction, cross over Henfold Lane and on to Mill Road. On your right is Fourwents Pond Car Park on Holmwood Common and the end of the ride. There is an option to continue your ride by cycling around the Common (Ride 16, Extension 2, page 172).

EXTENSION

As you make your way through Newdigate, turn left on to Kingsland following the Surrey Cycleway. You will follow this road, which changes its name to Trig Street halfway along, for 1.5km. Turn left on to Misbrooks Green Road and continue along here for 1.4km. As the road bears around to the right, you will see a sign for **Dorking Brewery** (⊘ dorkingbrewery. com), which sells its beers from a taproom to drink in or take away: turn left on to Temple Lane if you fancy a little detour to investigate. Once you pass the brewery signs, you will be on Vicarage Lane and the outskirts of Capel. At the T-junction, cross over The Street where you will see the **Church of St John the Baptist** and The Crown pub in front of you. As you enter the churchyard, the yew tree to your left, surrounded by a fence, is believed to be about 1,700 years old. A village legend claims that a ghost will appear to anyone who is prepared to walk around the tree a hundred times at midnight. The church itself dates to the 1200s, with one of its oldest features being in the chancel, where two small figures are seen, one dressed in red kneeling next to a desk. These are John Cowper, a patron of the church, and his wife. The Crown pub (closed Mon) sells a selection of local beers as well as a range of meals. To return to the ride, follow the route back the way you came until you reach Newdigate and turn right on to Village Street.

THE ESSENTIALS

GETTING THERE By train, the nearest stations to the start/finish point are Holmwood (2.55km; 1 hour 6 minutes from London Victoria) or Dorking (6.30km; 50 minutes from London Waterloo). By car, to get to Fourwents Pond Car Park (Holmwood Common), take the Mill Road exit off the Horsham Road (A24).

FACILITIES There are no public toilets on the ride.

WHERE TO EAT

Six Bells, Village St, Newdigate, RH5 5DH; ✆ 01306 631276; ⌂ sixbellsnewdigate.com. This 16th-century village pub sells a selection of local beers (as well as well known brands) and serves a range of meals and a small selection of sandwiches. Check out the side room which contains a rare chain-suspended log fire. **£–££**

The Surrey Oaks, Parkgate Rd, Parkgate, RH5 5DZ; ✆ 01306 631200; ⌂ thesurreyoaks.com. Some of this building dates to the 14th century although it didn't become a pub until 1650. A wide range of food is available including main meals, light bites, sandwiches and panini. The pub has three pétanque (or boules) pistes in the garden which, along with the equipment, can be hired. **£–££**

The Half Moon, 73 The Street, Charlwood, RH6 0DS; ✆ 01293 863414; ⌂ thehalfmooncharlwood.com. There has been a pub on this site for hundreds of years: watch your head if, like me, you are a little on the tall side, as some of the ceilings are quite low. Full meals and lighter bites such as sandwiches are available. If you sit outside the front of the pub, you can see a house opposite that dates to around 1400. Considering how long there has been a pub here, no ghosts or ghostly goings on have been reported! **£–££**

18 MERSTHAM LOOP

START/FINISH	Merstham Railway Station
DISTANCE/TIME	26.3km/2hrs
DIFFICULTY/TERRAIN	② Paved roads and downhill to start then following cycle routes and country lanes; a moderate climb near the end; a crossing over a busy A-road, travelling along another A-road for a short distance, and an off-road trail
SCENIC RATING	④ Spynes Mere Nature Reserve, Outwood Windmill, country pubs, and historic churches and villages
SUITABLE FOR	MTB, gravel or hybrid
CYCLE ROUTE	NCN21, Surrey Cycleway
MAPS	OS Explorer 146 (1:25 000)
KOMOOT REF	1158987911

↑ Outwood Windmill (David Lyon/A)

This ride starts in the village of Merstham, where one of the world's oldest railways used to finish. You will also pass by three churches, two of which date back to the Norman era. In addition, you can tick off one of Surrey's castles as well as passing by Outwood Windmill and the Spynes Mere Nature Reserve.

THE ROUTE

Turn right out of ❶ **Merstham Station** and head along Station Road North. Cross over the High Street (A23) on to Old Mill Lane. Follow this road as it bears to the left and then turn left on to Quality Street. This has nothing to do with the sweets but was named after a play by J M Barrie (he of *Peter Pan* fame) You will see some beautiful buildings along this road, some of which date back to the 16th century. Follow Quality Street until you are near its end, where, on your right you will see a town sign and a small seating area. Enter this to see what remains of the Surrey Iron

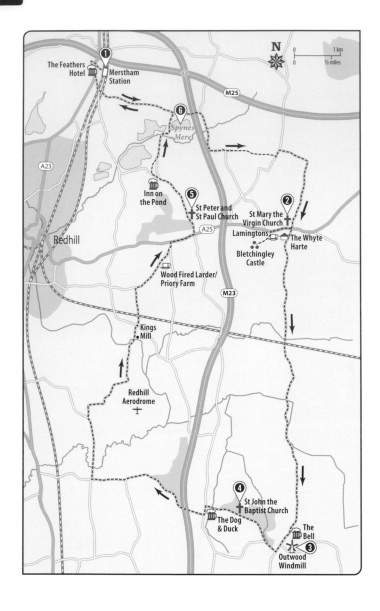

The Feathers Hotel
Merstham Station
1

7

M25

A23

N
0   1 km
0   ½ miles

6
Spynes Mere

Inn on the Pond

5
St Peter and St Paul Church
A25

2
St Mary the Virgin Church
Lamingtons
The Whyte Harte
Bletchingley Castle

Redhill

Wood Fired Larder/ Priory Farm

M23

Kings Mill

Redhill Aerodrome

4
St John the Baptist Church

The Dog & Duck

The Bell
3
Outwood Windmill

Railway (see box, page 187). Turn right on to High Street (A23) and, when you see the village clock, turn left on to School Hill. Follow this under the two railway bridges. After the second bridge, the road becomes Bletchingley Road. At the mini roundabout, take the first exit; at the next mini roundabout, take the second exit. Follow this road until you reach another mini roundabout, where you also need to take the second exit. Follow this road for another 1.8km; when it goes under the M23 and bears to the right, the name changes to Merstham Road. As it bears to the left the names changes once more, this time to Pendell Road.

On your left, you will see a sign for The Hawthorns School. Turn left here and take the second right, entering Water Lane. You will be joining NCN21. As the road bears to the right, continue straight on. The route is wide enough for one bicycle at a time, but beware of the undergrowth on either side, which includes brambles and stinging nettles and can encroach on the path. The path widens; pass around the gate you will soon come to. Go through the farm and then turn left on to Brewer Street. Turn right on to Place Farm Road, which is not only part of NCN21 (for a very short time) but also the Surrey Cycleway. This part of Bletchingley was once home to Anne of Cleves, fourth wife of Henry VIII. After the marriage was annulled, Henry gave Anne several properties including Bletchingley Place. The Tudor house is no longer in existence, but it was located along Place Farm Road.

As the road bears to the right, it becomes Church Lane. This becomes a single-track road for a while, and you may need to give way to oncoming vehicles. Near the end of the road, you will see the church of ❷ **St Mary the Virgin** on your right. You can enter the churchyard by going up the stairs and through the gate. The other option is to go up to the crossroads and take a right, entering the church via the road next to the Village Stores. The building is over 900 years old and has numerous information panels along the walls detailing the different parts of the church, as well as a very informative historical booklet. A highlight is the Grade I-listed Clayton Memorial (to the right of the altar). Sir Robert Clayton served as Lord Mayor of London, MP for Bletchingley and President of St Thomas' Hospital in London. You will also see a portrait of South African bishop

Desmond Tutu who was the assistant curate at the church in the mid-1960s. When you come out of the church, cross over the High Street (A25), where you can stop off in The Whyte Harte Hotel (which dates to the 14th century) for some refreshment. At the time of publication, the rooms were not available to book as the hotel has been going through a period of refurbishment. If you wish to take the extension to Bletchingley Castle (see below), now is the time to turn right on to High Street. Otherwise, take a left and then immediate right on to Outwood Lane.

You will be on Outwood Lane for the next 5.7km as well as continuing to follow the Surrey Cycleway. From Bletchingley, this is mostly a downhill ride, passing only the occasional building. Once you cross the bridge over the railway line, you will be travelling 3.7km until the next turn. When you notice the road going slightly uphill and past The Bell Inn, you will be on the outskirts of Outwood village, although this ride does not take you into the village itself. Continue past the pub, and the trees and hedges that line the roads will soon be replaced by open space. On your left, you will see ❸ **Outwood Windmill**.

This Grade I-listed building was built in 1665 and local lore has it that the glow of the Great Fire of London could be seen from the top; however, as the city is 40km from here, the windmill is not very tall and the Surrey Hills are in between the two locations, I will leave you to make your own mind up about whether it is true or not. It was still a working post mill until 1996. Unfortunately, it was damaged in gales between 2012 and 2013 and has been closed to the public ever since. You can get a good view of the windmill from the road but please don't try to enter the property as it is private land. Ride past the rusting beacon and turn right on to Miller's Lane, then right again on to Brickfield Road. On your right is Outwood Common, an 800ha site which has numerous paths to explore if you have the time.

Further along on the right you will see ❹ **St John the Baptist Church**. Built in 1869 and designed by the renowned Victorian architect William Burges, it is a relatively new church compared to the majority visited in this book. The churchyard has a unique gravestone: instead of the name of the deceased, it has a carving of a tractor and the inscription 'I am gone

SURREY IRON RAILWAY

Predating the first locomotive railway by two years, the Surrey Iron Railway was opened in 1802 with the track starting in Wandsworth and originally finishing in Croydon. Both Wandsworth and Croydon were in Surrey before the boundaries of what constituted London started to change at the end of the 1800s. The railway was designed to carry goods such as coal, manure, lime and fuller's earth. The line had L-shaped cast-iron rails and carried horse-drawn wagons. By 1805, the railway extended down as far as Merstham, just north of the current station but now under a section of the M23. Looking to modernise, the line asked George Stephenson, inventor of the standard gauge used by most railways around the world today, to supply a locomotive. He refused because he didn't believe the rails would support the weight of the engine. The line was eventually bought out by another railway company who were looking to use some of the route for their own trains. This horse-drawn railway has left a legacy, though: if you use the London Trams network between Mitcham Junction and just north of Waddon Marsh, you will be following the route once taken by the Surrey Iron Railway.

into the fields to take what this sweet hour yields'. Look out for a framed notice at the back of the church dating to 1898 which details the fees for services such as marriage and burials. The cost to a non-parishioner for a brick or stone vault is a bit pricey compared to the other services.

From the church, continue along Brickfield Road until you reach the T-junction. Turn left on to Prince of Wales Road and, after the Dog & Duck pub, turn right on to Green Lane. Continue along here for 2.4km, passing over the M23. The road changes name to Axes Lane. Turn right on to Mason's Bridge Road and follow this for 1km before turning right on to Kings Mill Lane. You have now left the Surrey Cycleway.

As you make your way along Kings Mill Lane, Redhill Aerodrome will appear on your right. Built in 1933, the aerodrome was home to several RAF fighter squadrons during World War II. Today, it is used for a range of commercial services as well as being a base for the Kent Surrey Sussex

Air Ambulance service. Further along the road, you will see a sign for **Kings Mill**. The white building to the right of the sign was a mill. Built in the mid-1700s, the mill was powered by Redhill Brook (which you pass over just before the building); it milled grain to produce flour for about 200 years. It ceased operations in the 1960s and today houses several businesses, none of which is related to milling.

At the T-junction, turn right on to Kings Cross Lane and then an immediate left on to Bower Hill Lane. Passing under the railway lines, the road will incline upwards; near the top, it will become quite steep. As you pass the sign for Hogtrough Lane, the road bears to the right and becomes Sandy Lane. At this point, you will be cycling downhill – but don't go too fast as you might miss the entrance to **Priory Farm** (see below). After you pass the farm, there is another upwards incline and, when you reach the T-junction, turn left on to Mid Street. At the next junction, turn right on to High Street (A25) and you're in Nutfield. This road can be busy and it's too narrow to have a dedicated cycle lane; however, you will be riding on it for less than 500m. Look out for The Queen's Head pub on your right, shortly after which turn left on to Church Hill. You will soon clear the treeline and see on your right the church of ❺ **St Peter and St Paul**.

It is believed there was a church on this site in Saxon times, but it was replaced by a Norman stone building, some of which still survives to this day. As you enter the churchyard, look for a memorial on the left wall of the lychgate which is dedicated to the memory of members of the Nickalls family who gave their lives in the two world wars – a poignant reminder of the sacrifices some families made in those conflicts. The church can be entered through the west door – if, like me you are fortunate enough to get in: the church closes its doors most of the time because of previous thefts of historical items. This is a shame, because it's another lovely church. One of its most interesting features is the stained-glass window in the east wall, in which the angels are shown with pink wings. The story goes that this caused quite a stir when they were installed in 1890: some of the congregation event went to worship in another church because they felt the colour of the wings was inappropriate. This window was designed by artist Edward Burne-Jones and produced by noted decorative arts manufacturer Morris & Co.

Not long after the church, the road changes name to Nutfield Marsh Road. Look out for the sign for the **Inn on the Pond** pub. The building dates to the mid-1600s and is well worth a visit. It is located just off the road, next to a pond, and on certain days Nutfield Cricket Club play on the field next door. After the pub sign, turn right following the blue sign for NCN21. You will soon see a sign for Mercers Farm and 'Private Property', but it is fine to ride through here. Go around the gate and you will be cycling through a field full of crops. Keep following the route until you reach a fence and a noticeboard. Beyond this fence is ❻ **Spynes Mere**, another location managed by the Surrey Wildlife Trust. This former sand quarry is home to many birds (such as greylag geese and sand martins) and insects (damselflies and dragonflies). If you fancied a quick dip, you would be disappointed: swimming is prohibited because the water is deep and there are patches of quicksand.

Follow the route until you reach the next gate. Pass through this and turn left. You are now back on Bletchingley Road. Retrace your ride for 1.75km and, at the Merstham Clock, turn right on to Station Road South. Follow this until you arrive back at Merstham Station.

↑ Spynes Mere in Nutfield (Ross Hamilton)

EXTENSION: BLETCHINGLEY CASTLE

Built in the first hundred years after the Norman invasion of 1066, excavations suggest that **Bletchingley Castle** was not built in the motte-and-bailey style common at the time. It was most probably a fortified country house. The castle was destroyed around 1264 during the Barons' War between Henry III and Simon de Montfort. To visit what remains, at the end of Church Lane, after the church of St Mary the Virgin, turn right on to High Street (A25) and travel along here until you turn left on to Castle Square. The road branches into two but in between them is a footpath. Walk along the path (it is not suitable for bikes) until you reach a gap in the treeline. Up the slope is a clearing and the site of the castle (/// bring.loudly.elite). The view looking south is incredible and it is easy to see why a defensive structure was placed here. To return to the route, ride back the way you came.

↑ The view from Bletchingley Castle (Ross Hamilton)

THE ESSENTIALS

GETTING THERE By train, Merstham Station is a 35-minute journey from London Victoria on the Brighton line. By car, the station is just off the A23 near Redhill.

FACILITIES There are public toilets at Merstham Station which can be accessed when it is manned, but only by passing through the ticket barriers.

WHERE TO EAT

Feathers Hotel, 42 High St, Merstham, RH1 3EA; ✆ 01737 645643; ⌂ pubanddining.co.uk. Dating to the 1800s, this pub is no longer a hotel, but it does serve a wide range of main meals as well as a selection of sandwiches. **£–££**

Lamingtons, 25 High St, Bletchingley, RH1 4PB; ✆ 07751 405020. This award-winning tea shop serves several lovely and very reasonably priced homemade cakes as well as a selection of light bites. The menu includes other homemade items such as soup and a quiche of the day. I recommend the ham and salad panini. It also doubles up as a gift shop. **£**

Wood Fired Larder, Priory Farm, Sandy Lane, South Nutfield, RH1 4EJ; ✆ 01737 823304; ⌂ prioryfarm.co.uk. Sandwiches, toasted panini and cakes as well as other sweet treats are available on this family-run farming estate. Wood-fired pizza is served Thu–Sun. The farm shop has a wider selection of food and drinks, including their estate gin. **£**

19 LINGFIELD LOOP

START/FINISH	Lingfield Railway Station
DISTANCE/TIME	22.2km/2hrs
DIFFICULTY/TERRAIN	① Back lanes and minor roads, with some moderate inclines
SCENIC RATING	⑧ Rolling farmland, a yew tree at least 1,500 years old, historic churches and an 18th-century poachers' prison
SUITABLE FOR	Road bike, MTB, electric bike, gravel or hybrid
CYCLE ROUTE	Yew Tree Way and Surrey Cycleway
MAPS	OS Landranger 187 (1:50 000)
KOMOOT REF	899526049

↑ The Cage lock-up and hollow oak in Lingfield (Ross Hamilton)

Y ou will be riding along a series of country roads including sections of the Yew Tree Way and Surrey Cycleway. You will pass numerous farms, woods, handsome churches, and the historic village of Lingfield. Located near the borders of Kent and East and West Sussex, the route is relatively flat but does have some inclines. This can be combined with Ride 21 (page 210).

THE ROUTE

Leave ❶ **Lingfield Station** and ride up to the T-junction at the end of the road. Turn right on to Station Road but be careful as the foliage makes this a bit of a blind corner. This is also Yew Tree Way, one of Surrey County Council's designated cycle routes around the county. The road changes name to Crowhurst Road before you reach the next junction. Turn right and then an immediate left, back on to Crowhurst Road, which you will be following for the next 2.9km. You will soon cross a bridge called Crowhurst Waste Bridge. It lives up to its name: there can be a distinctive whiff in the air as it is next to a water treatment plant.

Look to your left for a sign indicating you are entering **Crowhurst**. The name comes from 'crow's wood', as this area was once a forest. The first mention of the village dates to the 1100s with the building of St George's Church. As you ride through the village, look right to see the Parish Council garden. As well as an England flag hanging from the village sign, you will also see an Estonian one, the latter in honour of Leo Luksepp, an Estonian who settled in the village during World War II. He sought to foster a sense of community which Crowhurst has embraced and maintained even after his death.

After the Parish Council green, you will soon see a building in the Tudor style, with on its gate the words 'North Lodge' and 'South Lodge'. Behind here is Crowhurst Place, a Grade I-listed house which cannot be visited as it is privately owned. Once you pass Pikes Lane, the road changes name to Crowhurst Village Road. At Park Road, there is another name change to Crowhurst Lane. The road has a slight incline but once you reach the top, ❷ **St George's Church** is on your left.

The churchyard has a yew tree that is believed to be 4,000 years old, but 1,500 years is more likely. It was listed as one of the '50 Great British Trees'

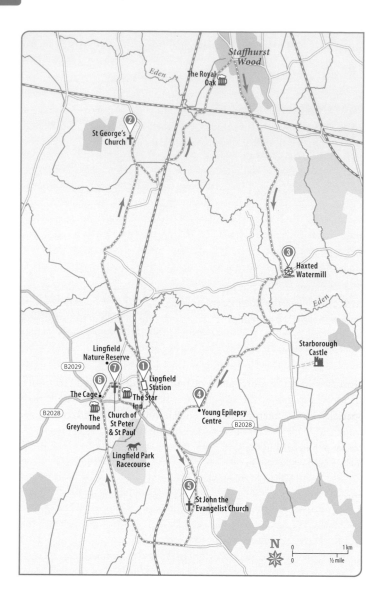

Staffhurst Wood

Eden

The Royal Oak

St George's Church ②

Haxted Watermill ③

Eden

Starborough Castle

Lingfield Nature Reserve

B2029

The Cage ⑥ ⑦

① Lingfield Station

The Star Inn

Church of St Peter & St Paul

B2028

The Greyhound

④ Young Epilepsy Centre

B2028

Lingfield Park Racecourse

⑤ St John the Evangelist Church

N

0   1 km

0   ½ mile

during the Queen's Golden Jubilee in 2002. The interior of the tree has been hollowed out and a door installed; it once had a table inside which could seat up to 12 people. The door is still there but the table has long gone. The church is not always open but if you catch it when it is, look for a wall painting behind the altar; if the light is right, the sunshine reflects off the golden stars to quite stunning effect. On the floor in front of the chancel is a Latin inscription dedicated to the memory of Richard Chomley who died in 1634. It claims he had strong moral principles which was approved by the public voice, but unfortunately I have been unable to find out more about this individual. The font could be older than the church itself and might be from the Saxon era, but this has been hard to prove.

Come out of the church and head back the way you came along Crowhurst Lane. Turn left on to Park Road, following the sign for Limpsfield and Oxted. Continue along this single-track road until you reach the T-junction. Turn left on to Caterfield Lane following the sign to Oxted. You will be on this road for 2.6km, passing under the railway (twice) and over the River Eden. As you pass under the second railway bridge, the road has a gentle incline. As you near the end of this road, you will see **The Royal Oak** on your right (see below). On your left past the pub is Great Earls Wood. Turn right on to Dwelly Lane and you will be riding past Staffhurst Wood. (It is at this junction that you have a slight crossover with the most southerly point of Ride 21, page 210.) Both sites are managed by the Woodland Trust and are designated Sites of Special Scientific Interest (SSSI) through having documented continuous woodland cover for over a thousand years. This woodland is known for its carpet of bluebells in the spring and is home to six rare species of moth, including the lead coloured drab.

As you continue on Dwelly Lane for 3.6km you are on part of the Surrey Cycleway. A good deal of this road, especially in Staffhurst Wood, is downhill, but once you cross the railway bridge it levels off. At the T-junction, turn right on to Haxted Road. On your right at the base of the slope, you will see a distinctive white building with a red post box built into the wall. Next to the post box is a sign that says 'Building of Historical Interest'. That is because this was the ❼ **Haxted Watermill**. A working mill from the 14th to the mid-20th century, it once housed a museum, bar and brasserie. At the time of writing, it is none of these things and now looks to be a private residence.

Cross over the River Eden once again and take a left on to Water Lane, leaving the Surrey Cycleway but rejoining Yew Tree Way. In 800m, turn right on to St Pier's Lane which you will be on for 2.6km. For most of its length, this is a single-track road so be careful of motor vehicles coming in either direction. You will see a welcome sign for the ❹ **Young Epilepsy Centre**. The centre has buildings (some of which are architecturally beautiful) from different eras and that is because it has been here since 1897. The centre started teaching agricultural skills to men with learning or physical disabilities, and continued its work with adults, including soldiers who had suffered brain injuries in World War I. The centre began

↑ Bluebells in Staffhurst Wood (Philip Bird LRPS CPAGB/S)

working with children in 1904 and, since 2001, it has been known as the National Centre for Young People with Epilepsy. At the end of the road, turn left on to Racecourse Road (B2028).

Take the next right on to Dormans Road, following the sign to East Grinstead and Dormansland. At the next junction, turn right on to Dormans High Street. Keep following the road until you see, on your left, the second pub on this ride by the name of The Royal Oak (currently open from Thursday to Sunday), which provided a refreshing pint on my last visit. On the opposite side of the road is the Village Store and Post Office. Established in 1865, this is a very old building, which I discovered when I banged my head on the low ceiling. Luckily, I still had my cycle helmet on. It's a useful stop for supplies, or somewhere just to sit outside relaxing on their bench. They have a coffee machine and serve light bites,

WHY ARE THERE SO MANY YEW TREES IN CHURCHYARDS?

The yew tree can live for hundreds, even thousands, of years and it grows well on the chalk and limestone soils found in Surrey. It was seen as a sacred tree in pre-Christian religions as it was believed that it would purify the dead as they made their way to the underworld. Yew trees were planted at places of worship and, when Christianity arrived on these shores, the earliest churches were built on the religious sites once used by pagans. Christians may well have favoured the yew tree in churchyards because of the toxicity of its bark, needles and seeds. This would have prevented cattle from grazing on the church grounds, thus not disturbing the bodies below. Yews were a good source of wood for the longbow – so successful in helping to win the Battles of Crécy and Agincourt – but it is unlikely that the churchyard yews were used for such a purpose, being on sacred ground.

↑ The old yew tree in St George's churchyard in Crowhurst (Ross Hamilton)

and they will also charge your phone while you wait. The red telephone box outside the shop adds to the charm, although these days it houses a defibrillator.

Just along from the village shop is ❺ **St John the Evangelist Church**. Unlike most churches in this book, the doors to the main church are closed unless the building is in use. The church was built in accordance with the wishes of a local landowner, William Henry Kinnaird Gibbons, who bequeathed in his will the sum of £500 for a church to be built near his Lingfield estate. A small chapel dedicated to St Andrew is open daily for prayer and meditation. Around the back of the church is a memorial garden, which rewards a moment spent there, if only for the spectacular view looking towards Lingfield.

Come out of the church and continue along Dormans High Street. As the road slopes downwards, turn right on to Dormans Station Road. This is a nice downhill to ride but be mindful of vehicles coming the other way. Dormans Station is on your right; because it doesn't have a car park, the roadside gets used instead. I don't know why the station has a different name from the village it serves. It might be because there is Dormans Park to the south and the name Dormans implies that it serves more than one Dorman settlement. As you pass the station, the road becomes Blackberry Lane; after 730m, turn right following the sign to Lingfield and Godstone. This road is still called Blackberry Lane; at the next junction, turn right on to East Grinstead Road. Pass over Eden Brook and you will soon see a sign for **Lingfield**. The village advertises itself as historic: you can see why as you make your way around.

At the mini roundabout, take a left on to Plaistow Street and then a right on to Vicarage Road. It is on this corner that you see ❻ **The Cage** (there is another such structure Charlwood: see Ride 17, page 179). This small Grade I-listed building was built in 1773 and was a one-room prison described as 'a lock-up for the temporary repose of miscreants'. There is an ancient, hollow oak next to The Cage, age unknown. Behind The Cage is Gunpit Pond, said to have been created when material was dug out to help with road construction. It is also quite a nice place to sit beside and relax while watching its colony of ducks. Continue down Vicarage Road and you will pass Glebe Close as the road bears around to the right. Look for a wooden gate on your left: this is the entrance to **Lingfield Nature Reserves** (⌂ lingfieldreserves.org.uk), which cover 10ha and have a wide range of environments including meadows and wetlands.

At the T-junction, turn right on to Church Road. Take the next right and you will be entering Lingfield Old Town. The first building is Pollard House, another Grade I-listed building, which dates to the 15th century and was once a butcher's shop. This short street has several interesting buildings along it. Check out the display on the wall opposite Pollard House for more information on what they once were. From here, make your way to the end of the street and the **❼ Church of St Peter and St Paul**. This is the third Grade I-listed building in Lingfield, with some of the stonework in the lower sections of the west wall dating to the Saxon era. There is much to see here, but of particular note are two tombs inside the church. The first, directly in front of the altar, is the last resting place of Sir Reginald de Cobham (1382–1446) and his second wife, Anne. The second, to the left of this, is the tomb of an earlier Sir Reginald de Cobham (1295–1361). This Cobham fought at the Battle of Crécy and was made a Knight of the Garter by Edward III.

Make your way back through the Old Town and turn right on to Church Road. Follow this until you reach the T-junction. Turn left on to Town Hill (B2028) and follow this until you reach Station Road. Turn left here and continue along the road

↑ Killing time on Lingfield Railway Station (Peter Trimming/WC)

until you reach the sign for Lingfield Station. A right here takes you to your destination.

THE ESSENTIALS

GETTING THERE By train, Lingfield is 51 minutes from London Victoria. By car, Lingfield Station can be reached via the Eastbourne Road (A22), Newchapel Road (B2028) and then Station Road.

FACILITIES There are public toilets on Godstone Road in Lingfield and Dormans High Street in Dormansland. Other toilets in Lingfield can be found on the station and inside the Church of St Peter and St Paul.

WHERE TO EAT

The Royal Oak (also known as The Grumpy Mole), Caterfield Lane, Oxted, RH8 0RR; 𝒫 01883 722207; ⟁ thegrumpymole.co.uk/oxted. This pub is well worth a visit for the view from the back garden alone. A wide selection of menus is available, from full meals to light bites such as sandwiches, panini and wraps. **£–££**

The Greyhound, Plaistow St, Lingfield, RH7 6AU; 𝒫 01342 832147; ⟁ greyhoundlingfield. co.uk. The pub dates to the early 1600s. Its menu includes a selection of main meals (including b/fast), sandwiches, salads and jacket potatoes. **£–££**

The Star Inn, Church Rd, Lingfield, RH7 6AH; 𝒫 01342 832364; ⟁ thestarlingfield.co.uk. Located opposite Lingfield Old Town, it has a wide selection of mains but there are some light bites as well, including sandwiches and nibbles. I recommend the cheesy garlic ciabatta. (See also *Accommodation*, page 228.) **£–££**

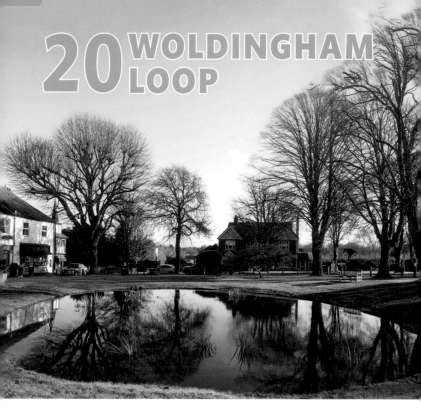

20 WOLDINGHAM LOOP

START/FINISH	Woldingham Railway Station
DISTANCE/TIME	27.5km/2¼hrs
DIFFICULTY/TERRAIN	② Two steep climbs and some fast downhills; one busier-than-normal B-road
SCENIC RATING	⑧ Stunning views across the North Downs, country lanes and historic churches
SUITABLE FOR	MTB, gravel, hybrid or road bike
CYCLE ROUTE	NCN21
MAPS	OS Explorer 146 and 147 (1:25 000)
KOMOOT REF	899575354

↑ Tatsfield village pond (James McGregor 33/S)

On this ride, you will be going up Botley Hill, the highest point on the North Downs. The ride also takes you past the site of a house once rented by anti-slavery campaigner William Wilberforce, along with great views and historic churches, all while riding down country lanes. I suggest this is a ride for the more experienced cyclist owing to the two climbs and the busier-than-normal B-roads.

THE ROUTE

Leave ❶ **Woldingham Station** by going through the exit on the western platform, where you will see a small car park. Follow the road until you reach a barrier across the road, but this will rise automatically when you get close enough to it. Just past the barrier, you will come to a T-junction. Turn left here on to Woldingham School Drive, a single-track road. Until you reach the top of Gangers Hill in 6km time, all the roads you are on are either single-track or at best narrow roads. This is part of NCN21 and you will be on this road for 3.2km. This is arguably the most picturesque ride from a station in this book. There are very few buildings for the first 1.3km of this ride as you pass through farmland. Take the first left turning, past a clump of trees, and you should see an alpaca in the field on your left.

Come back to Woldingham School Drive and, once you pass over the speed bump, there is a sign for **Woldingham School**. NCN21 passes through here, but do not deviate from the route as anywhere else is out of bounds for non-school users. The road has several speed bumps along it; watch out for pedestrians as there can be a lot of them on the road depending on the time of day. As you make your way through the school grounds, a hedge lines the left hand side of the road; once it changes to a tree lined route, look left and you will see a building with a blue plaque. This was the site of Marden Park Manor, which was for a short while the home of anti-slavery campaigner William Wilberforce. The house is not the original one he resided in as it was rebuilt in 1911.

Leaving the school buildings behind you, pass through a set of gates, although you are still within the school grounds. On your right, you will see one of the school's latest projects: a vineyard, which has been planted to make better use of some of their 280ha site and to generate income for future bursaries. As you leave the school grounds, you will come to another barrier. Unlike the one next to the station, this one does not open and you will need to take the path to your left. Ahead of you is a house. Turn left here, leaving NCN21 but joining Quarry Road. This has a steady incline but, if you get a chance to look through the treeline to your right, the view across the North Downs is well worth stopping for.

As you come to the end of Quarry Road, there is a sharp left turn on to Gangers Hill. This is a steep hill and has a blind corner where the road bears to the right as soon as you join it. Be mindful of cars coming in the opposite direction because you are on a narrow road. You will be on this hill for 2.1km and, at its steepest, there is a 9% gradient. As the road bears to the right for a second time, you will see a path into **Marden Park**. These were once part of the grounds of Marden Park Manor but are now

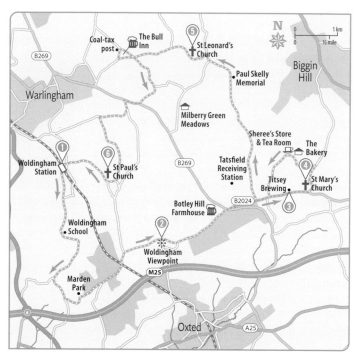

managed by the Woodland Trust. If you decide to go exploring here, you will need to walk as cycling is prohibited. At /// bumpy.nature.aware, there is a view over the North Downs that is well worth stopping for. You may also be lucky and see roe deer eating the vegetation up against the fence of Marden Park as I did on one of my rides. When you reach the T-junction, turn right on to The Ridge.

You will be on The Ridge for 2.8km but, after 1km, you will see a car park to your right. This is the ❷ **Woldingham Viewpoint** (/// moved.closed. margin) and it is also well worth stopping off at. From here, you can see as far as East Sussex and you get to look down on Old Oxted (see Ride 21, page 213). The information board says you may see buzzards and kestrels flying around ready to swoop on their prey. I saw a pair of the latter on my last trip here. The only thing that spoils this view is the metal fence. Turn right back on to The Ridge and continue until the next T-junction.

Turn right on to Limpsfield Road (B269) and you will soon reach a roundabout. Take the first turning following the sign to Westerham/ Tatsfield. You are now on Clarks Lane (B2024), which you will follow for 1.9km. As you make your way along this road, you will see several broadcasting towers above the hedges. These are the remains of the **Tatsfield Receiving Station** (see box, page 206), which are located on Botley Hill, the highest point on the North Downs. Although Clarks Lane is a B-road, it is a lot busier than most of the ones you have travelled down so far in this book. The road has a gentle descent, and you will see, on your left, the entrance to ❸ **Titsey Brewing** (closed Mon–Wed). Not only does it sell delicious beer, but also breakfast, burgers and sides throughout the day. The view from the brewery across the North Downs is spectacular. Just past the brewery is a carving: the swirling seed emblem of the Surrey Hills Area of Outstanding Natural Beauty (see page 169).

Take a left turn off Clarks Lane on to Church Hill. Just before this turning, you pass over what was once the London to Lewes Roman road; Clarks Lane follows it for a short time just after the turning for Church Hill. In contrast to the gentle downhill you have just experienced, this is an incline which becomes steep near the top. When you reach the summit, you will see ❹ **St Mary's Church, Tatsfield** on your left. One gravestone

TATSFIELD RECEIVING STATION

Tatsfield Receiving Station was built in 1929, its original purpose being initially to monitor radio and then subsequently television broadcast transmissions. Being located so high up in the landscape made it perfect for this operation. It was said that, on a clear day, St Paul's Cathedral in central London could be seen some 20 miles away. It was important that broadcasts stayed on their assigned frequency so that they did not interfere with other users. In 1939, it became part of the BBC Monitoring Service, which was designed to give the British Government access to foreign media, and was very useful during World War II as it was able to gather vital information from occupied countries. During the Cold War it would pick up signals from early spacecraft such as Sputnik 1. The site was closed around 1974 and the work transferred to Crowsley Park in Oxfordshire. Even though some of the buildings remain, they are in ruins and the area is out of bounds.

in the churchyard is for Commander Robert Radcliffe Cooke (who died in 1924 at the age of 41, having served in the Royal Navy in World War I) and looks most unusual as his sword and belt are carved into it. The church itself dates to the Norman era, with the nave and two small windows in the north wall dating to that period. Another feature to look out for is a low window in the south wall in a quatrefoil shape which could be a leper window. These were designed so that, during the Middle Ages, people with leprosy could watch mass from outside the church – because, in those days, the disease was seen as a punishment from God.

Church Hill descends after the church; take the next left turning on to Ship Hill. There is a bit of an uphill as you make your way along this road. As it bears to the right, you enter the village of Tatsfield with its village green. Here, you will find the pub Ye Old Ship, **The Bakery** restaurant with its distinctive tower (see *Accommodation*, page 225), **Sheree's Store & Tea Room** (see below) and the village pond. I quite like the fact that the signpost on the green does not point to other nearby settlements but rather to locations within the village, such as the church, playing field and village hall.

As you pass the green, the road becomes Approach Road, which you will follow for 1.3km. At the T-junction, turn right following the sign to Croydon/Warlingham. You will once again be on Clarks Lane (B2024) but this time travelling in the opposite direction. Take the next right turning on to Beddlestead Lane, which you will be on for 3.4km. The road descends for most of that distance and it is easy to pick up a lot of speed. Do be mindful as this is a single-track road and you need to be careful of vehicles going in either direction. As you make your way down the road, you may see a small white and yellow marker on your right (/// ruler.tasty.ranch). This is dedicated to the memory of Paul Skelly, an avid cyclist and fundraiser, who loved cycling this road. Beckenham Rugby Cyclists have an annual 640km challenge in January in his honour. The road bears to the left and then you will be going uphill once again. At the T-junction, turn left on to Heslers Road and then an immediate right on to Fairchildes Road.

Quickly take a left turn on to Church Lane, which is narrow, and follow it for 2km. However, in a little over 200m, after the road takes a sharp right, look out for the slip road, also on the right. This will take you to ❺ **St Leonard's Church, Chelsham**. The church, which was mentioned in the Domesday Book (even though the oldest parts of the current building date to the 13th century), is rarely open outside of services and this has been the case every time I have tried to visit. However, in the churchyard, you will see some leaping boards and a mortsafe. In the early 19th century, mortsafes were cages used to protect the recently buried from having their bodies stolen from the grave. During this period, surgeons were eager for bodies to practise

↑ The gravestone of Commander Robert Radcliffe Cooke in St Mary's graveyard, Tatsfield (Ross Hamilton)

on, and the body snatchers were happy to help them out. The nefarious trade died out by the mid-1800s due to changes in the law.

As you make your way down this road, the number of trees (especially on your right) increases because you are passing Ledgers Wood. Managed by the Surrey Wildlife Trust on behalf of Surrey County Council, it is best visited in spring when the bluebells and primroses are in bloom. After you have been on Church Lane for 2km, turn right on to Ledgers Road. On your left is Chelsham Pond, which is a nice spot to relax next to. A little bit further is a left turn that will take you to **The Bull Inn** (see below). At the crossroads, look ahead to see a coal-tax post (see Ride 15, page 161). Turn left on to Chelsham Road, and then the next left on to Chelsham Common Road. At this point, you will briefly be riding along NCN21. Turn right to get back on to Ledgers Road, which is narrow, and stay on it for 1.2km. When you reach the T-junction, turn right on to Limpsfield Road (B269). This can be a busy road, but you are not on it for long as you need to take a left turn on to Slines Oak Road. This road has a fast decline and it is easy to pick up a good deal of speed here, too. However, if you go too fast, you might miss the spectacular view which appears when you clear the treeline. As the road bears to the right, it changes name to Halliloo Valley Road. The road has an incline, which continues until you turn left on to Lunghurst Road, which you will follow for 1.7km.

Turn right on to Croft Road; when you reach the end of this road, you will see ❻ **St Paul's Church** on your left. Again, here is a church that does not open very often, and it's quite modern compared to most in this book, being consecrated in 1934. It does not have a graveyard but there is an area of remembrance next to the understated war memorial. Turn right on to Station Road, which you will be on for 1.2km. The road is downhill all the way to the station and the end of this ride. Be careful along this stretch of road, though, as the decline is 11% at one point.

THE ESSENTIALS

GETTING THERE By train, Woldingham is 36 minutes from London Victoria. By car, Woldingham Station is 6.5km from Junction 6 of the M25, via the A22 and then heading along Woldingham Road.

FACILITIES Toilets are available on Woldingham Station when the ticket office is open.

WHERE TO EAT

Botley Hill Farmhouse, Limpsfield Rd, Warlingham, CR6 9QH; ✎ 01959 577154; ⬦ botleyhill-farmhouse.co.uk. You have two options on this site. There is the 16th-century pub (closed Mon & Tue) which serves a selection of main meals and also sandwiches at lunchtime. The second option is the Sheep Shed which specialises in lighter bites including cream teas (open 7 days). £–££

Sheree's Store & Tea Room, The Parade, Tatsfield, TN16 2AQ; ✎ 01959 928181. Sells a selection of cakes (the staff informed me that the Eccles cakes are very popular) along with hot and cold drinks. If the weather is good, you can sit outside next to the village pond. Water refill and toilets are available here. Closed Tue and between noon and 12.30 every day except Sun. £

The Bull Inn, Chelsham Common, Warlingham, CR6 9PR; ✎ 01883 627735; ⬦ thebullinnchelsham.co.uk. Located in Chelsham Common, The Bull offers different menus depending on the season. A selection of main meals, sandwiches and panini is available along with hot and cold drinks £–££

21 HURST GREEN TO OXTED

START	Hurst Green Railway Station
FINISH	Oxted Railway Station
DISTANCE/TIME	28.5km/2½hrs (Extension: 3.4km, 30min round trip)
DIFFICULTY/TERRAIN	② Undulating in places with one large climb; crossing a busy A-road more than once
SCENIC RATING	④ Historic house and churches while riding along country lanes
SUITABLE FOR	MTB, gravel, hybrid or road bike
CYCLE ROUTE	Surrey Cycleway, Yew Tree Way
MAPS	OS Explorer 146 and 147 (1:25 000)
KOMOOT REF	899288127

↑ Titsey Place (Tony Watson/A)

This route takes you along several country lanes, some of which go right to the Kent border, while passing through Staffhurst Wood and Limpsfield Common. There are historic churches, including one with a 2,000-year old yew tree. On the extension, you can visit a country house and gardens.

THE ROUTE

Exit the car park of ❶ **Hurst Green Station** and turn right on to Greenhurst Lane. At the junction, turn right once again, continuing to follow Greenhurst Lane. You will cross a bridge going over the railway line and then take the second right on to Oast Road. Take the next left on to Church Way and, on your right, you will see ❷ **St John the Evangelist Church**. Built between 1912 and 1913, this church has a couple of features

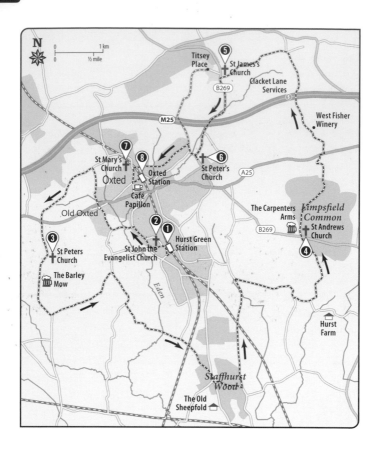

to look out for inside. St John the Evangelist is associated with eagles and there is a lovely wooden carving of one on the wall. The other feature is an Ethiopian Coptic processional cross; there are not many of these in the UK and this is the only one I have seen on my travels in Surrey.

Continue along Church Way until you come to the crossroads. On the opposite side of the road is the Hurst Green war memorial, which must be one of the most understated I have ever seen, being just a small wooden board with the names of those who gave their lives in the two world wars. It also lists the civilian causalities, which is unusual. Turn right on to Woodhurst Lane. The road has an incline; as you near the top, turn left on to Spring Lane, a single-track road sloping downwards on which it is easy to pick up speed. Be careful of vehicles coming in the opposite direction. The road takes a left after you have crossed the River Eden and in front of you is what used to be Oxted Mills. Mentioned in the Domesday Book, the mills were still in use up until 1951 for milling flour at which point they closed and the machinery was removed. The building was later converted into offices. Opposite is the mill pond: a nice place to sit and watch the wildlife, which on my visits seemed to be mostly ducks.

As you come to the end of Spring Lane, there is a small fenced-off area on your left (/// lakes.quiet.handy). I find this to be a great place to stop and look at the wonderful view to the south. At the T-junction, turn right on to Beadles Lane. There is a small uphill but, after that, you make your way on a nice gentle slope downwards until you reach another crossroads. You are now in **Old Oxted**. The road you need to cross is the High Street and ahead of you is The Old Bell pub, which was originally built as a hall in the Elizabethan era. This isn't the only old building on the High Street: turning right, you will see references to some other buildings' former

↑ Oxted mill pond (Ross Hamilton)

purposes, such as 'The Old Post Office' and 'The Old Bakery'. None of these businesses survive, but there are three more pubs in historic buildings to visit if you are so inclined.

Crossing the High Street, you are now on Brook Hill. Continue along this country road as it passes under the A25 and changes its name to Sandy Lane. At the T-junction, turn left on to Barrow Green Road. Continue on this road for 1.6km until you meet the A25 again. You will need to cross straight over this at the roundabout, but be warned: it is a busy road. There is a traffic island to your left if you do not feel comfortable riding here. Once you are across, you will be riding down Tandridge Lane.

As the road bears to the right, you will see a sign for Tandridge on your left. The next left turning will take you to ❸ **St Peter's Church**. Whenever I have visited this Grade I-listed 11th-century church it has been locked, but it is still worth visiting the churchyard for the yew tree, which is believed to be over 2,000 years old. The church has asked that visitors do not get too close, not only to protect the tree for future generations but to ensure the surface roots under the canopy are not damaged. As you exit the churchyard to rejoin Tandridge Lane, there is another lovely view on the opposite side of the road (/// giving.paying.model). As you continue your ride, you will see two signs on your right. One is for the wonderfully named Jackass Lane and the second is to warn of a 10% gradient fast approaching. This is downhill and is along a mostly straight road, but don't go too fast as you might miss **The Barley Mow** (see below). The road bears to the left and then comes to a T-junction, at which you turn left on to Southlands Lane following the sign for Oxted and Hurst Green. You have now joined the Surrey Cycleway.

Follow the road for 1.6km before turning right on to Gibbs Brook Lane. You will soon need to take a left on to Popes Lane, following the sign for Merle Common and Edenbridge, as well as the brown Surrey Cycleway sign. On this road, you will pass over the River Eden again. Once you pass Holland Road (which is on your left) and go under the railway line, the name of this road changes to Merle Common Road. There is an incline here approaching the T-junction, at which you turn right on to Red Lane. Take the next left on to Dwelly Lane, following the sign for Crockham Hill and Pains Hill. You are not on Dwelly Lane for long as you need to

WHY IS THERE SO MUCH SANDY SOIL IN SURREY?

All of Surrey is composed of layers of sedimentary rocks, which are formed by the deposition of minerals or organic particles. These include the Bagshot Beds, a loose sandstone formed as deposits from postglacial rivers. Glaciers in the UK did not reach as far south as Surrey, but as the water drained out from the ice sheets at the end of the last ice age (approximately 11,700 years ago) the sands and gravels were washed out from the ice sheets to the north. This has led to poor soils, a feature of most of northwest Surrey. In central and southern Surrey, the soil is made up of clay and chalk. Northwest Surrey was therefore not amenable to crop growing on a large scale, so Surrey, in comparison to adjacent counties, was sparsely populated in the Iron Age. However, where the chalk of the North Downs meets the clay of the Weald, freshwater springs provided a water source. This, and the grasslands that grow on the chalk, provided a suitable habitat for grazing animals and clay for cultivation of some crops. The heathlands were and still are undeveloped due to these poor soils.

take another left, this time on to Staffhurst Wood Road, leaving the Surrey Cycleway. It is at this junction that you have a slight crossover with the most northerly point of Ride 19 (page 192).

You are now passing through **Staffhurst Wood**, a site managed jointly by Surrey County Council, the Woodland Trust and Surrey Wildlife Trust. If you have the time, there are several walks you can follow through the forest. Here you may see some of the 200 plant species that have been recorded within its borders, which include bluebells and beech trees, some of the latter having fallen, being at the end of their lifespan. These fallen trees now provide a home for the wildlife that feeds on the rotting remains. As for fauna, you may see birds such as sparrowhawks and red kites; butterflies such as the brimstone, mammals such as the long-eared bat; and amphibians including the great crested newt. Cycling is not recommended on these woodland tracks as they are designated for walkers.

At the end of Staffhurst Wood Road, turn left on to Grants Lane, joining the Yew Tree Way. You will be on this road for 2.3km, first passing over a railway bridge and, not long after, taking a right on to Itchingwood Common Road, following the sign to Crockham Hill. After 1.2km, you will pass by handsome houses on your left, and a pond on your right with a duck house on it, as the road bears to the right. After an incline, turn left on to Swaynesland Road and follow it until you reach a pair of open gates. This is Trevereux Hill; the sign says that this is a 'no through road', but you can travel along it on a bike. You will be on this road for 1.55km and there is quite a steep climb as you near its end.

At the end of Trevereux Hill is a crossroads. Pass over Kent Hatch Road (B269) and on to Moorhouse Road and follow it for 1.9km. Immediately on your right is ❹ **St Andrew's Church**, built in 1896 with the bell-tower added in 1902, each of these dates being commemorated in stone on the side of the church. This is another church I have not been able to enter on my visits here. If you look closely at the second buttress on the western wall, you will find a symbol scratched into one of the stones: a short line at the top running from east to west and two further lines coming down at 45° angles from its centre. Maybe it is there to ward off evil spirits. Ahead of you is the village of Limpsfield Chart and to your left is **The Carpenters Arms** (see below). Limpsfield Chart once had the distinction of having a windmill the blades of which moved clockwise (most have blades that move anticlockwise). Unfortunately, the mill was demolished in 1925.

As you continue along Moorhouse Road, you will be passing through **Limpsfield Common**. The land was donated by the Gower family (see extension below) to the National Trust. A visit to the Common might reward you with a sight of roe deer or a common lizard. There are also some rare insects such the girded mining bee. I found Moorhouse Road pleasant to ride along as, for the most part, it slopes downwards. At the end of the road, you will need to turn right on to Westerham Road (A25). Although earlier we could get away with just crossing the A25, now we need to cycle along it for a short time, although there is a pavement you can follow if you do not feel comfortable on this busy road.

Turn left on to Clacket Lane and follow it for 2.4km. Regular drivers along the southern section of the M25 might recognise the name from the eponymous service station. This is a single-track road so be mindful of vehicles coming from either direction. The first building you will see on your left is an old stable that houses **West Fisher Winery**, a UK wine producer (open Thursday to Sunday from noon). The grapes are sourced from all over the southeast and southwest of England, and wine can be bought by the glass if you decide to drop in. Wine tastings need to be booked in advance but there is also a selection of local beers and soft drinks if wine is not your tipple. All their products are available to be taken away as well.

The road inclines upwards, and you will cross a bridge over the M25 where you will see Clacket Lane Services to your left and right. You will soon come to a T-junction, where you turn left on to Pilgrims Lane. This could well be the most beautiful road I have ridden while researching this book. As you first turn into it, you can see the road snake off into the distance with the gorgeous Surrey countryside before you. You will be on this road for 1.6km and, at its end, you will see a church on your right: ❺ **St James's**, a Grade II-listed church in Titsey which was built by local squire Granville Gower in the 19th century. If you are lucky enough to gain entry (it is only open from mid-May to mid-September, Wednesday, Saturday and Sunday afternoons), you will see memorials and tombs for the Gower family inside (see extension below).

Turn left on to Titsey Road (B269) and follow it for 2km as you make your way to the village of Limpsfield, going under the M25 on your way. This is one of the busier roads on this ride. As you enter the village, the road takes a sharp left and, on the left, you will see ❻ **St Peter's Church**. Built in the 12th century it is now Grade I-listed, and is notable for the number of musicians buried in its churchyard. These include composer Frederick Delius and the Harrison sisters. One of the stained-glass windows is dedicated to St Cecilia, patron saint of musicians on account of the amount of musical talent in the churchyard. There is a rare leaping board, and the churchyard contains 77 different flowers (including cow parsley, salvia and oxeye daisy) and several trees, including a Lebanon cedar. Inside the church is the chest tomb of John Elphinstone, former governor of Madras (India) and member of the Privy Council under William IV.

To return to the route, go back the way you came and then go straight ahead on to Bluehouse Lane. You will be on this for 1.7km as you make your way into Oxted. As you pass under the railway line and over the pedestrian crossing, you will see ❼ **St Mary's Church** in front of you. Possibly mentioned in the Domesday Book of 1086, this building has areas dating to the 12th century. There are several interesting features within it, including brasses, tombs dating to the 1600s, and decorative memorials. However, what stood out for me was the stained-glass window dedicated to Edward Hoskins in which the angel has blue wings. This is also the only churchyard I have visited for this book where you could see some sheep. These are Soay sheep: they eat the grass to reduce the workload of those who manage the grounds. The sheep might come up to you, but visitors are asked not to feed them; be careful in lambing season as the rams may butt you to protect their young.

Come out of the church and head right down Church Lane. At the roundabout, turn left into Station Road West. Ahead of you is ❽ **Oxted Station** and the end of your ride.

EXTENSION: TITSEY PLACE

The land where Titsey Place is now located has a long history of occupation: ruins of a Roman villa have been found on the site. The estate was acquired in 1534 by Sir John Gresham, who had been Lord Mayor of London. The Gresham family crest was a grasshopper, which is why you will see the occasional reference to that creature while riding around this area. The last of Sir John's descendants would marry into the Gower family, a powerful family of nobles whose titles included the Duke of Sutherland. The house dates to 1775 and retains numerous Georgian features such as the main entrance hall and gallery bedroom. The gardens can also be visited and are designed to show how crops were harvested in the Victorian era. The café here is also worth a visit for its selection of homemade cakes, some of which have some rather interesting combinations of ingredients. One that was available on my visit was lime and courgette. Other more traditional café fare is also available such as toasties, panini and scones, as well as the usual hot and cold drinks.

To get there, you need to look for a sign for Titsey Place and Gardens when Bluehouse Lane bears to the left. Turn right here on to Water Lane and follow it for 1km. Here, you will see some more signs for Titsey Place. Turn right on to the estate's driveway and follow it for a further 840m. In the fields either side of the driveway, you may see some Sussex cattle from the Titsey Herd. That does mean that there are cattle grids to negotiate along the way. At the end of the driveway, you will see the entrance to Titsey Place as well as the café. The site is only open from mid-May to late September, and then only on Wednesday, Saturday and Sunday afternoons (for specific opening hours, check ⊘ titsey.org). To return to the route, go back the way you came.

THE ESSENTIALS

GETTING THERE By train, Hurst Green Station is 44 minutes from London Victoria. By car, Hurst Green Station is 6km from Junction 6 of the M25, via the A22 and A25, then heading south from Oxted along Rockfield Road, Wolf's Hill and Hurstlands.

FACILITIES Hurst Green and Oxted Stations have toilets which are open when the ticket office is open.

WHERE TO EAT

The Barley Mow, Tandridge Lane, Tandridge, RH8 9NJ; ✆ 01883 713770; ⊘ barleymowtandridge.com. This beautiful country pub is open from 08.00 every day with hot b/fasts at the w/end. There are bike racks at the side of the pub and a serving hatch around the back. Full meals and light bites are available. **£–££**

The Carpenters Arms, Tally Rd, Limpsfield Chart, RH8 0TG; ✆ 01883 722209; ⊘ carpenterslimpsfield.co.uk. Built in the 1800s, this pub specialises in main meals, although a selection of small plates, sides and light snacks is also available. Being at the start of the Limpsfield Community Cycle Route (there is an information board with details of the route opposite the pub), the pub has a bike tool station nearby (on the corner where Tally Rd meets Post Office Row). **£–££**

Café Papillon, 54 Station Rd West, Oxted, RH8 9EU; ✆ 01883 717031; ⊘ cafepapillon. co.uk. Located next to Oxted Station, the café serves a selection of main meals and light bites including hot as well as cold drinks. **£ ££**

ACCOMMODATION

These hotels, B&Bs, self-catering units, holiday parks and campsites have been chosen due to their location on or near the cycle routes (the numbered circle in each listing shows which route/s they are close to). Accommodation is listed by area in descending price order, and prices are based on rates per night during the summer high season. Check, though, as some have cheaper off-season rates.

£ up to £50   **££** £50–£100   **£££** £100+

WEST SURREY

Asperion Hotel, 73 Farnham Rd, Guildford, GU2 7PF; ✆ 01483 579299; ⌂ asperionhotels. com; ❷ ❼. Located in the heart of Guildford, there are 15 rooms (11 dbls, all en suite; 4 sgls, 3 en suite). Rooms come with TV, b/ fast, Wi-Fi & tea- & coffee-making facilities. Prices can fluctuate with demand. Booking directly includes b/fast & free parking. Closed for 2 weeks over Christmas. **£££**

Bel & The Dragon, Jumps Rd, Churt, GU10 2LD; Tel: 01428 605799; ⌂ belandthedragon-churt. co.uk; ❶ ❷. This restored country pub (with a beautiful garden) has 18 rooms (13 in the main building & 5 in the Cottage annexe). Dbl, twin & sgl rooms (inc. 2 family & 2 premier) are available & are named after Jane Austen characters due to her Surrey connections. A 15% discount & a complimentary gin are offered if booked directly. Rooms come with TV, b/fast, Wi-Fi & tea- & coffee-making facilities. The hotel also provides free parking. Even though no ghosts have been recorded here, there have been reports from members of staff of hearing strange noises when the building is quiet. **£££**

The Bulls Head Inn, The Street, Ewhurst, GU6 7QD; ✆ 01483 277447; ⌂ thebullsheadinn. co.uk; ❽. Located in the village of Ewhurst, this Edwardian inn has 5 king-sized en-suite rooms & 1 suite which can sleep up to 4. Rooms come with TV, b/fast, Wi-Fi & tea- & coffee-making facilities. The hotel provides free parking & a secure cycle storage area. **£££**

Bush Hotel, The Borough, Farnham, GU9 7NN; ✆ 01252 715237; ⌂ farnhambush.com; ❷ ❸. Welcoming guests since 1618, the recently renovated Bush Hotel is an independent, family-run business located in the centre of historic Farnham, with 94 rooms (dbls & twins), all en suite. Rooms come with TV, Wi-Fi & AC. Advisable to book direct. Free parking, & secure cycle storage, but you need to ask for this in advance. **£££**

Cowshot Manor Barn, Queens Rd, Brookwood, GU24 0NX; ✆ 01483 797799; ⌂ cowshotmanor.com; ❹ ❺. This stunning

16th-century barn conversion was once home to animals as well as people. The manor refers to an area & not a specific house. One king-sized dbl bed with shower, kitchen, lounge & even a study. Free Wi-Fi, parking & cycle storage facilities. 3-night min stay. **£££**

The Crown Inn, The Green, Petworth Rd, Chiddingfold, GU8 4TX; ☏ 01428 682255; ⌀ thecrownchiddingfold.com; ❻. Dating back to the 15th century, The Crown Inn has 8 en-suite rooms (7 dbls, some with 4-poster beds, & 1 sgl). The rooms come with TV, Wi-Fi, b/fast & tea- & coffee-making facilities, as well as free parking. The prices are seasonal; book direct for the best deal. This is a building of great historic interest & there is a fantastic history of the inn on the website, which is well worth a read. **£££**

Hammonds Glamping, Lower Hammond's Farm, West Horsley, KT24 6JP; ☏ 07849 086460; ⌀ hammondsglamping.com; ❿ ⓫. There are 10 tents: 5 for 6 people, 4 for 4, & 1 basic that sleeps up to 5 (bring your own sleeping bags for this, even though they can be hired). On site parking, toilets, showers, firepit & picnic table. A refreshment trailer is open in the morning & evening, serving a range of snacks as well as hot & cold drinks. On site activities include table tennis, a children's play area & an old London Routemaster bus to explore. Open May–Sep; min 2 nights' stay; visitors must bring their own cooking equipment. **£££**

Hascombe Accommodation, Hatch Cottage, Markwick Lane, GU8 4BE; ☏ 07856 646655; ⌀ hascombeaccommodation.co.uk; ❾. Housed

in a converted stable, this luxury self-contained property has 1 room with dbl bed, kitchenette & bathroom. TV, internet access, on site parking & a secure cycle storage area. Basic b/fast is provided. **£££**

The Merry Harriers, Hambledon Rd, Hambledon, GU8 4DR; ☏ 01428 682883; ⌀ merryharriers.com; ❻. Dating from the 16th century, The Merry Harriers has 15 en-suite rooms in 3 different buildings, each with their own features which are fully explained on the website. Each room comes with Wi-Fi, TV & tea- & coffee-making facilities. Free parking & a secure area for a limited number of bikes. An unusual feature of this location is to go trekking with llamas which can be booked through the pub. There are rumours that there is a ghost in Room 2. **£££**

Oxenford Gatehouse, Elstead Rd, GU8 6LA; ☏ 01628 825920; landmarktrust.org.uk; ❸. Designed in the mid-1800s by famed architect Augustus Pugin as a gatehouse to Peper Harow House, this beautiful building is located on a working farm. It has 2 rooms (1 dbl, 1 twin), kitchen & social area. The building was designed to evoke the Middle Ages & has a spiral staircase as well as an open fire should you stay during a chilly period (logs are provided). Min 4-night stay (Mon–Fri) or 3-night stay (Fri–Mon). Parking available on site. **£££**

The Percy Arms, 75 Dorking Rd, Chilworth, GU4 8NP; ☏ 01483 561765; ⌀ thepercyarms. net; ❼ ❽. This country pub in the village of Chilworth has a southern African feel to it. There are 5 rooms (each with an African name), 3 with en suite, 2 with roll-top slipper baths. Included with the rooms are TV, Wi-Fi & b/fast. The room rates are more expensive on Saturdays. Off-street parking & cycle storage area. **£££**

Rookery Nook B&B, The Square, Shere, GU5 9HG; ✆ 01483 209382; ⌂ rookerynook.info; ❿ ⓬. Located in the beautiful village of Shere, this 15th-century building can sleep up to 4 people in 2 dbl rooms. These rooms share a bathroom. There is a TV lounge as well as period features such as creaking doors & wonky floorboards to add to the charm. There is a hearty, complementary b/fast & the owners try their best to source all their b/fast ingredients locally. There are homemade cookies to be sampled with the tea & coffee. There is parking, but it is in a public area & cannot be guaranteed, as well as a secure area for bikes. Owner Chris is a keen cyclist himself. **£££**

Tor Hatch, Sandy Lane, Shere, GU5 9QL; ✆ 07767 230338; ⌂ torhatch.co.uk; ❿ ⓬. 8 rooms based in 3 buildings, each with a dbl bed. This property occupies 2ha of land & each of the buildings has a kitchen, Wi-Fi, TV & on site parking. The main building has access to a tennis court, yoga sessions & a swimming pool. The pool is only available to use in the summer months. The 3 buildings can be booked separately or as one package. Secure cycle storage available. **£££**

Vaughans B&B, The Square, Shere, GU5 9HG; ✆ 01483 203165; ⌂ vaughansbnb.co.uk; ❿ ⓬. The original building was completed in 1580, but there have been several additions made over the years. The apartment is a separate space from the main house & contains 2 dbl bedrooms plus a sofa bed in the living room, as well as a kitchen with a microwave & crockery for up to 6 people. Wi-Fi is available & there is a TV in the living room. Check out the 'Out & About' section of their website as 2 pubs (The William Bray & The White Horse) offer discounts to Vaughans' guests. There is a secure area to store cycles. Vaughans has 2 MTBs which can be borrowed free of charge. Fans of the 2006 film *The Holiday* may recognise the square where Vaughans is located. **£££**

Walnut Tree Cottage, Vann Lane, Hambledon, GU8 4EF; ✆ 07891 875679; ⌂ walnuttreecottage.uk; ❻. This 17th-century cottage has 1 room which contains a king-size bed, en-suite shower, Wi-Fi, TV, tea- & coffee-making facilities & the option of an additional bed. B/fast is cooked by one of the owners & the eggs are freshly laid by the resident chickens. Bikes can be stored in their lockable shed & there is on site parking. Additional £10 charge for any children over 5. **£££**

De Vere – Horsley Estate, Ockham Rd South, East Horsley, KT24 6DT; ✆ 01483 917075; ⌂ devere.co.uk/horsley-estate; ❿ ⓫ ⓭. This majestic 19th-century building was designed by Charles Barry (who also designed the Houses of Parliament) & is well worth a visit even if you are not staying there. It has 180 en-suite rooms (dbls, twins, sgls) in more than 1 building. Each room has Wi-Fi, TV & tea- & coffee-making

facilities. Bikes can be stored in reception which is manned 24hrs a day. You can even book a room in the tower (which is said to be haunted). **££–£££**

Frensham Pond Hotel & Spa, Pond Lane, Churt, GU10 2QD; ℘ 01252 795161; ⊘ frenshampondhotel.co.uk; ❶ This former coaching inn overlooking Frensham Great Pond has 53 rooms (dbls, twins & sgls, all en suite). Rooms come with TV, AC, Wi-Fi & tea- & coffee-making facilities. Free parking & a secure cycle storage area. It also has a spa if you wish to pamper yourself before &/or after the ride, but that is an additional charge. **££–£££**

Lion Brewery, 104 Guildford Rd, Ash, GU12 6BT; ℘ 01252 650486, 07790 900373; ❹. Despite its name, this is not a brewery. It has 8 rooms with sgl, dbl, twin & trpl options & a family room that can house 5 people. Rooms come with TV, Wi-Fi & tea- & coffee-making facilities. Free parking & a secure area for bikes. Bookings can be made by phone. **££–£££**

The Stag on the River, Lower Eashing Lane, Lower Eashing, GU7 2QG; ℘ 01483 421568; ⊘ stagontherivereashing.co.uk; ❸. Backing on to the River Wey, this 17th-century pub has 7 rooms (1 family, 6 dbls; all en suite). Free parking available, & bikes can be kept in

↑ The beautiful village of Shere (Richard Jemmett/D)

rooms. Prices are seasonal & it is cheaper to book direct. **££–£££**

The Talbot, High St, Ripley, GU23 6BB; ✆ 01483 225188; ⌂ thetalbotripley.com; ❾ ⓫. This building dates to 1453 & still has many original features, including low door-frames. There are 43 rooms in the original coaching inn & the newer Ripley Wing, including dbl, twin & sgl bed options & all are en suite. Rooms include Wi-Fi & tea- & coffee-making facilities, with b/fast included. Free parking, & cycle storage available on request. There is a room dedicated to Lady Hamilton (no relation): she & Horatio Nelson were said to have stayed in this inn during their extramarital affair. Two ghosts have also been reported to haunt it. It was also a destination for those pioneers of bike riding completing the Ripley Ride (see Ride 8, page 106). **££–£££**

St Augustine's Abbey, Sampleoak Lane, Chilworth, GU4 8QR; ✆ 01483 899360; ⌂ chilworthbenedictines.com; ❼ ❽. Christian monasteries have offered accommodation throughout their history, & St Augustine's is no different. The guesthouse has 3 sgl rooms, & 1 dbl. Men & women of all faiths (or none) are welcome to experience monastic life, but only men can join the monks in their refectory; women must eat in the guesthouse. Meals can be provided but self-catering is an option. A min payment of £50 is requested for your stay but the monks ask you donate to the running costs of the monastery according to your means. **£–£££**

The Half Moon, High St, Ripley, GU23 6AN; ✆ 01483 224380; ⌂ thehalfmoonripley.co.uk; ❾ ⓫. This 18th-century inn has 6 rooms (2 dbls & 4 twins): 5 are en suite with one of the twin rooms having a private shower. Rooms come with TV, Wi-Fi & tea- & coffee-making facilities. The inn does not have its own car park but there is free parking on the green behind the pub. Cycle storage available in the secure courtyard out the back. Book direct for the best price. **££**

Hatsue Guest House, 17 Southwell Park Rd, Camberley, GU15 3PU; ✆ 07791 267620; ⌂ hatsueguesthouse.com; ❹. This guesthouse has 5 en-suite rooms (2 dbls, 2 sgls, 1 twin). They come with TV, Wi-Fi & tea- & coffee-making facilities. Free parking. Secure cycle storage available on request. B/fast is included with fresh eggs provided by the resident chickens. **££**

The Squirrel Inn, Hurtmore Rd, Godalming, GU7 2RN; ✆ 01483 860223; ⌂ the-squirrel. co.uk; ❸. Rooms are available in the 16th-century cottages next to the pub. 7 en-suite rooms (5 dbls, 2 sgls). 1 additional sgl is not en suite. There is parking, & bikes can be kept in the room. Cheaper to book direct. **££**

The Station, 2 Station Rd, West Byfleet, KT14 6DR; ✆ 01932 336353; ⌂ thestationwestbyfleet.co.uk; ❾. Bookings for this pub, right next to West Byfleet Station, can only be completed through booking.com. A link on the pub's website will take you there. The pub has 9 rooms, the twin & trpl rooms en suite. The sgl rooms have shared bathrooms.

Open all year (except Christmas Day). Free parking in front of the pub but this cannot be reserved. Bikes can be stored in the pub's back garden which has a locked gate. **££**

Chantry Wood Campsite, Halfpenny Lane, Guildford, GU4 8PZ; ⌂ guildford.gov.uk/chantrywoodcampsite; ❼. Located at the edge of Chantry Wood on the North Downs, this basic campsite has parking, piped water, firepits & chemical toilets but no showers. Enclosed on three sides by woodland & hedgerows, you will be able to sample the views of Albury Valley & Chilworth. Bookings are made only through the website & you need to do so at least a week in advance. Open all year (except Christmas & New Year). **£–££**

Basingstoke Canal Authority Campsite, Canal Centre, Mytchett Place Rd, Mytchett, GU16 6DD; ⌘ 01252 370073; ⌂ hants.gov.uk/thingstodo/countryparks/basingstokecanal/canalcentre/camping; ❹. The website is Hampshire County Council's, who run this Surrey campsite. Bookings need to be made by phone but information about the site can be found on the webpage. Washing facilities & toilets available 24hrs a day for campers. Free

parking. Camper-vans, motorhomes & trailers can be brought on site. **£**

Horsley Camping & Caravanning Club Site, Ockham Rd North, KT24 6PE; ⌘ 01483 283273; ⌂ campingandcaravanningclub.co.uk; ❾–⓫ ⓭. Welcoming members & non-members alike, this site is located next to Horsley Lake, if you fancy a bit of fishing during your stay. Facilities include Wi-Fi, showers, toilets, children's play area & recreation room. Bring your own tent or rent out one of the site's 4 glamping options. There is limited on site parking. 2-night min stay in Jul & Aug. Open Mar–Dec. **£**

Waggoners Campsite, Puttenham Rd, Farnham, GU10 1HP; ⌂ waggonerscampsite.co.uk; ❷. This environmentally friendly campsite is on the Hampton Estate. It has showers, wash huts, drinking water, firepits & logs, & compostable toilets. There are instructions on the website on how to use the toilet which are not only essential but humorous too. No access to electricity on the campsite. Open only Apr–Oct as well as Easter. Vehicles can be parked on visitors' pitches. **£**

EAST SURREY

The Bakery, Westmore Green, Tatsfield, TN16 2AG; ⌘ 01959 577605; ⌂ thebakeryrestaurant.com; ⓴. Based in the old village bakery, there are 7 dbl rooms, all en suite. Rooms come with b/fast, Wi-Fi, TV & tea & coffee making facilities. Free parking &

secure cycle storage also available. Book direct for the best price. **£££**

Blackbrook House Country B&B, Blackbrook Cottages, Blackbrook Rd, Dorking, RH5 4DS; ⌘ 01306 888898; ⌂ surreybandb.co.uk; ⓰ ⓱. This country house has two en-suite

dbls with tea- & coffee-making facilities. Wi-Fi, free parking & secure cycle storage. You can also enjoy the on site garden & use the tennis court. Closed for 2 weeks over Christmas; booking direct is advisable. **£££**

Denbies Vineyard Hotel, Denbies Wine Estate, London Rd, Dorking, RH5 6AA; ✆ 01306 876777; ⬡ denbies.co.uk; ⓭ ⓯. Located on the Denbies Wine Estate, the hotel is based in 2 buildings: the 19th-century Farmhouse (7 dbl en-suite rooms) & The Brokes (10 dbl en-suite rooms). They include Wi-Fi, TV, b/fast & tea- & coffee-making facilities. The hotel provides free parking & a secure cycle storage area. Vineyard tours are available from the visitor centre. There is also the Surrey Hills Brewery on site. **£££**

The Green Escape, Leith Hill, Dorking, RH5 5PA; ✆ 07590 693271; thegreenescape.co.uk; ⓬. This glamping site has 7 shepherds' huts & an indoor lodge. The huts contain 15 beds (dbls & sgls) sleeping max 22 people. The lodge contains cooking facilities & a dining area with crockery provided but you need to bring your own food. Open all year round with different rates depending on the season. No parking on site. A booking is for the whole site & not individual huts. **£££**

Hurst Farm, Dairy Lane, Crockham Hill, TN8 6RA; ✆ 01732 866516; ⬡ hurst.farm; ㉑. Just over the border in Kent, this estate has buildings dating back to the Middle Ages. Sleeps up to 10 guests with 4 en-suite rooms with dbl or twin options. There is a communal area which includes a kitchen as well an outdoor pool & tennis court which can be used in season. Off-street parking & a cycle storage area. Min 2-night stay Thu–Sun. **£££**

Hurtwood Hotel, Walking Bottom, GU5 9RR; ✆ 01306 730514; ⬡ hurtwoodhotel.co.uk; ⓫. Built in the 1920s, Hurtwood Hotel has 15 en-suite dbl rooms, each with TV, Wi-Fi & tea- & coffee-making facilities. B/fast inc.

↑ Decisions, decisions (Amanda Thompson)

Room rates vary depending on the time of year. They have a second site on the other side of the road called the Old School House, a self-contained cottage that can sleep up to 4 adults & 3 children. Book direct for the best price. Cycling experience packages can also be booked via the website. **£££**

The Old Sheepfold, Dwelly Lane, Edenbridge, TN8 6QG; ✆ 07803 010676; ⓓ theoldsheepfold.co.uk; **⓳ ㉑**. Located on the Surrey–Kent border, this converted shepherd's hut has 1 bed, shower, toilet & a kitchenette, but no cooking is allowed inside. A BBQ is available in the garden. B/fast, sourced from local farms, can be ordered at additional cost. Off-road parking & a secure cycle storage area. Check out the website for the different packages that are available. Min 2-night stay at w/ends. There is also a resident barn owl who you might be lucky to see on your visit. **£££**

The Plough Inn, Abinger Rd, Coldharbour, RH5 6HD; ✆ 01306 711793; ⓓ ploughinn. com; **⓮**. The Plough has 6 rooms, all dbls & all en suite. Each comes with Wi-Fi, TV, & tea- & coffee-making facilities, with b/fast inc. It also has its own micro-brewery on site, the Leith Hill Brewery, whose beers can be enjoyed in their lovely garden. Parking is available & cycle storage on request. **£££**

The Semaphore Tower, Chatley Heath, off Pointers Rd, KT11 1PQ; ✆ 01628 825925; ⓓ landmarktrust.org.uk; **⓫**. One of the last remaining semaphore towers in the south of England which once relayed messages from London to Portsmouth during the Napoleonic Wars. It is a beautiful setting with fantastic views from the higher levels, being surrounded by woodland. There are 2 rooms (1 dbl, 1 twin). Separate shower & bathroom, but this is an old building so accessibility could be an issue. Min stay 4 nights (Mon–Fri) or 3 nights (Fri–Mon). Free on site parking & bikes can be stored in the basement. **£££**

The Foley Hotel, 106 Hare Lane, Claygate, KT10 0LZ; ✆ 01372 462021; ⓓ thefoley.co.uk; **⓯**. This haunted former coaching inn has 17 en-suite bedrooms (a mix of twins & dbls). Prices vary depending on the season or events at Sandown Park Racecourse. Rooms come with TV, Wi-Fi & tea- & coffee-making facilities. Bikes can be kept in the 4 downstairs rooms (if not muddy) or the storeroom (the management stress they do not hold responsibility for anything that happens to bikes when they are on site). Free parking subject to availability. **££–£££**

Hartsfield Manor, Sandy Lane, Betchworth, RH3 7AA; ✆ 01737 835300; ⓓ hartsfieldmanor.co.uk; **⓰**. Dating from the 1860s & once used by the Canadian Army in WWII as a hospital, this converted country house has 50 en-suite rooms including dbls & sgls. Rooms come with TV, Wi-Fi & tea- & coffee-making facilities; 10% discount available when booking directly. Free parking & a secure cycle storage area. It also offers a cycle break package, details of which can be found on the website. **££–£££**

Milberry Green Meadows, Milbury Cottage, Beech Farm Rd, CR6 9QJ; ✆ 07943 992921; ⌂ milberrygreen.co.uk; ❷⓿. Stay in either their shepherds' huts (each sleeps 2) or bell tents (2 adults, 2 children) while enjoying the lovely view. The huts come with a cosy bed, kitchenette, shower, toilet & wood stove. The tents have communal showers & toilets. There is an on site games room for wet-weather days. B/fast supplied from local farms but needs to be ordered in advance. Parking available on site & secure cycle storage by arrangement. **££–£££**

The Red Lion & Cellar Room, Old Rd, Betchworth, RH3 7DS; ✆ 01737 843336; ⌂ theredlionbetchworth.com; ❶⑥. This 18th-century pub has 9 dbl rooms of various bed sizes including one suitable for families & 1 twin room. Each room has tea- & coffee-making facilities & TV. Free parking & a secure cycle storage area. The Cellar Room restaurant is a converted WWII bunker & there aren't many pubs that have a cricket club in the back garden. **££–£££**

Trumbles Guest House, Stan Hill, Charlwood, RH6 0EP; ✆ 01293 863418; ⌂ trumbles.co.uk; ❶⑦. This Victorian house has 8 en-suite dbl rooms but 2 can be converted to twin use. 2 have a kitchenette. Parking & secure cycle storage facilities available. **££–£££**

Westleigh, Farm Lane, Ashtead, KT21 1HP; ✆ 07850 224422; ⌂ escapetosurrey.com; ❶⑤. This guesthouse has 4 dbl rooms & 1 suite designed to sleep up to 4 people: 3 are en suite; 2 have a shared bathroom. Rooms come with TV, Wi-Fi & tea- & coffee-making facilities. Free parking & a secure cycle storage area are provided. B/fast is offered. Book directly for cheaper rates. **££–£££**

The Star Inn, Church Rd, Lingfield, RH7 6AH; ✆ 01342 832364; ⌂ thestarlingfield.co.uk; ❶⑨. This 1930s pub has 6 rooms in the upstairs area & 3 in their outside building. Dbl & twin rooms available as well as 1 family option to sleep up to 4. Each room is en suite with Wi-Fi, TV & tea- & coffee-making facilities. B/fast available. Bikes can be stored in the shed. Rooms not available 24–26 Dec. **££**

Embers Polesden Lacey, National Trust Campsite, Polesden Lacey Estate, Great Bookham, RH5 6BD; ✆ 0345 257267; ⌂ emberscamping.co.uk/campsites/polesden -lacey-surrey; ❶③. Located on the site of the Polesden Lacey estate, this National Trust-run campsite sits in 560ha of land in the Surrey Hills. Washrooms are available, along with a snack bar & each plot has a firepit. There is pizza oven, but you will need to order in advance. A bell tent & inflatable mattress can be hired so you don't need to bring your own. The site is open May–Sep. The camping fees include access to the Polesden Lacey House. Pricing is charged at a per-person rate. **£–££**

CYCLE HIRE AND REPAIRS

BIKE HIRE

Alice Holt Bike Hire, Alice Holt Forest, Bucks Horn Oak, GU10 4LS; ☏ 01252 940915; 🖥 southernebikerentals.co.uk; ❶. Based in the Alice Holt Visitor Centre, this hire shop has mountain & hybrid bikes for adults & children. They also have electric tourers & e-mountain bikes. Children's seats, tagalongs & trailers available. Hourly, half-day, full day & long-term hires with deliveries as well as pick-ups. Helmets, pumps & puncture kits are supplied for bikes going off site.

Cycling Collective, 1a St Martin's Walk, Dorking, RH4 1UT; ☏ 020 3148 6764; 🖥 thecyclecollective.cc; ❸ ❺ ❻. Performance road & touring e-bikes can be hired on half-day or full-day rates, but longer hires can be negotiated. Adult bikes only. Panniers, GPS, repair kits & helmets are included in the price. Coffee & cakes are available as well as bike fitting, repair service, sales & accessories. Closed Mon & Tue.

Just Pedal, Denbies Wine Estate, London Rd, RH5 6AA; ☏ 01306 885152; 🖥 justpedal.com/bikehire; ❸ ❺ ❻. Not a traditional bike hire shop but a test centre for Canyon bikes. Adult frames only, including road, hybrid, gravel & mountain varieties. Helmets can be hired but they recommend you bring your own. On site workshop for bike repairs. Closed Mon & Tue.

On Your Bike, Felbridge Forge, London Rd, East Grinstead, RH19 2BQ; ☏ 01342 777700, 🖥 onyourbike.com; ❿. Based just over the border in West Sussex, & hiring out hybrid as well as a range of road bikes. Accessories include lights, panniers & a seat pack containing a spare tube & tyre levers. Day & weekly rates available on the hybrid. Min 72hr hire for road bikes. Hires need to be booked a week in advance. On site workshop for bike repairs. Closed Mon & Sun.

Surrey Hills Bike Rental, The Little Shop, Walking Bottom, Peaslake, GU5 9RR; ☏ 01306 731639; 🖥 surreyhillsbikerental.co.uk; ⓬. Also known as The Riders Hub, they only hire out adult MTBs (electric & non-electric). All bikes must be booked in advance. Helmets can be hired but they recommend you bring your own. A day rate is standard but longer hires can be negotiated.

Surrey & Sussex E-Bike Hire, Faygate Lane, Horsham, RH12 4RF; ☏ 0204 558 3854; 🖥 electricbike-hire-surreysussex.co.uk; ⓮ ⓰ ⓱. Covering Surrey (& Sussex), they will deliver & pick up within 16km of Rusper (near Horsham). They have 2 bike types in adult sizes only: a touring hybrid & a mountain. Half-day, full-day & week hires available. The hire package includes a helmet, puncture repair kit, a lock & a basic first aid kit. Long-term hires come with the charging unit. Online booking only.

CYCLE SHOPS

Ace Bicycles, 218 London Rd, Guildford, GU4 7JS; ✆ 01483 302210; ⌕ acebicycles.co.uk; ❷ ❼. Run by Toby, a former professional mountain biker, they repair bicycles as well as sell them. Accessories also available. Closed Sun.

Head For The Hills, 43 West St, Dorking, RH4 1BU; ✆ 01306 885007; ⌕ head-for-the-hills. co.uk; ❸ ❺ ❻. Drop-in emergency repair service available for minor works. Bike sales & accessories also available. Closed Sun & Wed.

Hoops, Unit E, G Grovebell Industrial Estate, Wrecclesham Rd, Wrecclesham, GU10 4PL; ✆ 01252 448836; ⌕ hoopsvelo.com; ❶ – ❸. Bike repairs, sales & accessories. Closed Sun.

Horsley Cycles, Station Approach, East Horsley, KT24 6QX; ✆ 01483 284298; ⌕ horsleycycles. co.uk; ❿ ❸. Rather handily, this is located next to Horsley Station. Bike repairs, sales & accessories. Closed Sun & Mon.

Pedal Active, 5c Rectory Lane, Ashtead, KT21 2BA; ✆ 07932 038940; ⌕ pedalactive.com; ❺. Not only do they do bike repairs & sell accessories but you can get an on site sports massage (advance bookings only). Closed Sun.

↑ Denbies Wine Estate, Dorking (Ross Hamilton)

FURTHER INFORMATION

CYCLING ORGANISATIONS

Cycling UK ⊘ cyclinguk.org. One of the largest & oldest cycling membership organisations in the UK, founded in 1878 & formally the Cyclists' Touring Club, with lots of members' activities & cycling trips. The Surrey section of the website gives details of local clubs & groups.

Sustrans ⊘ sustrans.org.uk. The nationwide charity behind the National Cycle Network, with its excellent paths for cyclists & other users in towns, cities & the countryside around the whole of the UK. The website has detailed maps & recommended routes with helpful tips, as well as maps for sale.

APPS

These are a few of the best-known navigation apps (with offline maps to use wherever internet signal is unavailable). Useful in conjunction with this book as well.

Gmap Pedometer ⊘ gmap-pedometer. com. Useful for planning routes in advance, for cyclists & walkers. Covers footpaths & gives details of overall ascent/descent.

komoot ⊘ komoot.com. Ready-made routes worldwide for cyclists, runners & walkers, with downloadable route maps & offline

functionality. Its well-involved membership adds a community feel, with useful tips & feedback. Used in preparing all the routes in this book.

MapMyRide ⊘ mapmyride.com. A popular route tracker for cyclists, with route planning as standard, along with other functions.

Strava ⊘ strava.com. One of the big worldwide route trackers for runners & cyclists, with lots of features such as lifetime stats & challenges for the more competitive rider. Some features, such as route creator, only available to subscribers.

USEFUL WEBSITES

Forestry England ⊘ forestryengland.uk. The UK's forestry management service, which includes woodland around Witley & the Surrey Hills, with details of local activities & facilities. It's worth checking in advance if you plan to visit one of their forests, for updates on seasonal forestry work, during which some routes may be closed (eg: Alice Holt **❶**).

Public Toilets ⊘ publictoiletnearme.com. A map of the UK showing the sites of public toilets.

RSPB ⊘ rspb.org.uk. The nationwide bird charity has a presence on Farnham Heath & Bourne Wood, where it has succeeded in increasing the numbers of the rare Dartford warbler **❸**

Surrey Churches Preservation Trust ⌖ surreychurchespreservationtrust.org. This church preservation charity raises money to help secure the future of these historic buildings. They run an annual Ride & Stride fundraiser.

Surrey County Council ⌖ surreycc.gov. uk. Search the website to find out more about Surrey's Cycle Network & other routes throughout the county.

Surrey Wildlife Trust ⌖ surreywildlifetrust. org. A wildlife preservation trust that manages & protects nature reserves across the county. Many of the rides in this book (eg: Newdigate Brickworks ❸) cross land that they manage.

Visit Surrey ⌖ visitsurrey.com. The official visitor website for Surrey with a range of tips about what's on, where to stay, bike hire & cycle routes. (I'm not sure that the Surrey Wine Route is advisable by bike.)

FURTHER READING

Books on Surrey

A History of Surrey by Peter Brandon (History Press, 2022, 144pp). Surrey is not blessed with many books looking at its history, but this is concise yet comprehensive. This edition is an update from the 1977 original.

Roads Were Not Built for Cars by Carlton Reid (Island Press, 2015, 340pp). An excellent book on the early history of cycling, focusing on Britain & the USA. Deals with campaigns by cyclists for better roads as well as the links between bikes & the early years of motoring. The follow-up, *Bike Boom*, from 2017, is also well worth a read.

Bike books

The Big Book of Cycling for Beginners by Tori Bortman (Rodale Books, 2014, 290pp). Although published in 2014, this remains a valuable & comprehensive book covering everything from safe cycling to tips on buying your first bike, what to wear & the best nutrition for cyclists. US cycling consultant Bortman also offers confidence-boosting insights on the benefits of cycling for our physical & mental health.

Bike Repair Manual by Chris Sidwells (Dorling Kindersley, 2021, 176pp). A handy, pocket-sized manual with DK's trademark illustrations. With clear tips on practical maintenance, accessible even for complete beginners, it also includes an overview of different types of bike & accessory. For adults & children.

ACKNOWLEDGEMENTS

First, I would like to thank all the people who came out with me on these rides. Your companionship and feedback was greatly received. They were: Lynn Abrahams, Glenn Cain, Theresa Capel, Adam Conway, Kay Eggleton, Danny Francis, Andrew Hall, Sarah Hamilton, Justin Holder, Jo Kingston, Gemma Lineham and Nick Wilde. My biggest thank you goes to my old school friend Jason Gibbs, who joined me for at least ten of these rides (including some that did not make the book) in all weathers and in every part of the county. Your support and feedback was most appreciated. I would also like to thank Rosie Cooke, Aidan Elliott, Cindy and Graham Hancock, Olly Morrison and Helen Smith for all their help and guidance.

To Rob Marshall of komoot for talking me through the ins and outs of the app. To Elizabeth Rowley for her help with Surrey's geographical make-up; it was nice to know where and why there was so much sandy soil in the county, even though it did not make it any easier to ride through. To Elizabeth Burke and Gillian Lachelin at Ockham Church: thank you for opening the doors to your lovely church and giving me a personalised tour of the building. To Jamie at Giro in Esher for informing me about the Lovelace Bridges Trail.

To Roger Cansdale (Basingstoke Canal Society), Emily Caroe (Vann Garden), Dennis Cruickshank (Chairman of the Wonersh History Society), Oliver Fry (Surrey Wildlife Trust), Jackie Godfrey, Alan Johnson (Wey & Arun Canal Trust), Victoria Leedham (Hannah Peschar Sculpture Garden) and John Tagg (The Chiddingfold Archive) for supplying information regarding your respective organisations.

Thanks to the team at Bradt – Adrian, Anna, Claire and Neil – for giving me an opportunity to share my bike journeys from the lovely county of Surrey. A special thanks to Dean Bargh and Chris Reed, my very patient and supportive editors. I would also like to thank Huw Hennessy for the use of his material.

To all those whose names I don't have but who were happy to talk to me as I cycled past, giving me so much useful information about their local area. I am also grateful to all the historians for their informative work on

the churches I visited while researching this book. Apologies to anyone whom I have missed, but I thank you all.

Two special thanks to end with. To Geoff Attewell, not only for lending me your bike but for getting me back on mine after a few years of cycling inactivity. Lastly, to my wife Sarah, who not only joined me on some of these rides but also had to put up with a husband constantly in lycra, who, on more than one occasion, came home drenched and covered in mud.

↑ The Old Bell pub in Old Oxted (Ross Hamilton)

INDEX

Page numbers in **bold** indicate main entries; those in *italics* indicate maps.

Published in association with komoot
First edition published February 2024
Bradt Guides Ltd

31a High Street, Chesham, Buckinghamshire, HP5 1BW, England
www.bradtguides.com
Print edition published in the USA by The Globe Pequot Press Inc,
PO Box 480, Guilford, Connecticut 06437–0480

Text copyright © 2024 Bradt Guides Ltd
Maps copyright © 2024 Bradt Guides Ltd; includes map data © OpenStreetMap
contributors
Photographs copyright © 2024 Individual photographers (see below)
Project Manager: Chris Reed
Cover research: Ian Spick, Bradt Guides

ISBN: 9781804691359

British Library Cataloguing in Publication Data
A catalogue record for this book is available from the British Library

Photographs Photographers credited beside images and also those from libraries
credited as follows: Alamy.com (A); Dreamstime.com (D); Shutterstock.com (S);
Wikimedia Commons (WC)
Front cover Top: The River Wey, Guildford (Amartphotography/D); Bottom: Cyclists
on the towpath on the River Wey Navigation Canal at Byfleet (Peter Lane/A)
Back cover Hankley Common (Sarah Hamilton)
Title page Autumn view from the top of Box Hill (TS Corrigan/A)
Author photo by Andrew Hall

Maps David McCutcheon FBCart.S

Typeset by BBR Design, Sheffield
Production managed by Zenith Media; printed in the UK
Digital conversion by www.dataworks.co.in

THE BRADT STORY

In the beginning

It all began in 1974 on an Amazon river barge. During an 18-month trip through South America, two adventurous young backpackers – Hilary Bradt and her then husband, George – decided to write about the hiking trails they had discovered through the Andes. *Backpacking Along Ancient Ways in Peru and Bolivia* included the very first descriptions of the Inca Trail. It was the start of a colourful journey to becoming one of the best-loved travel publishers in the world; you can read the full story on our website (bradtguides.com/ourstory).

Getting there first

Hilary quickly gained a reputation for being a true travel pioneer, and in the 1980s she started to focus on guides to places overlooked by other publishers. The Bradt Guides list became a roll call of guidebook 'firsts'. We published the first guide to Madagascar, followed by Mauritius, Czechoslovakia and Vietnam. The 1990s saw the beginning of our extensive coverage of Africa: Tanzania, Uganda, South Africa, and Eritrea. Later, post-conflict guides became a feature: Rwanda, Mozambique, Angola, and Sierra Leone, as well as the first standalone guides to the Baltic States following the fall of the Iron Curtain, and the first post-war guides to Bosnia, Kosovo and Albania.

Comprehensive – and with a conscience

Today, we are the world's largest independently owned travel publisher, with more than 200 titles. However, our ethos remains unchanged. Hilary is still keenly involved, and **we still get there first**: two-thirds of Bradt guides have no direct competition.

But we don't just get there first. Our guides are also known for being **more comprehensive** than any other series. We avoid templates and tick-lists. Each guide is a one-of-a-kind expression of an expert author's interests, knowledge and enthusiasm for telling it how it really is.

And a commitment to wildlife, conservation and respect for local communities has always been at the heart of our books. Bradt Guides was **championing sustainable travel** before any other guidebook publisher. We even have a series dedicated to Slow Travel in the UK, award-winning books that explore the country with a passion and depth you'll find nowhere else.

Thank you!

We can only do what we do because of the support of readers like you – people who value less-obvious experiences, less-visited places and a more thoughtful approach to travel. Those who, like us, take travel seriously.

Bradt GUIDES
TRAVEL TAKEN SERIOUSLY